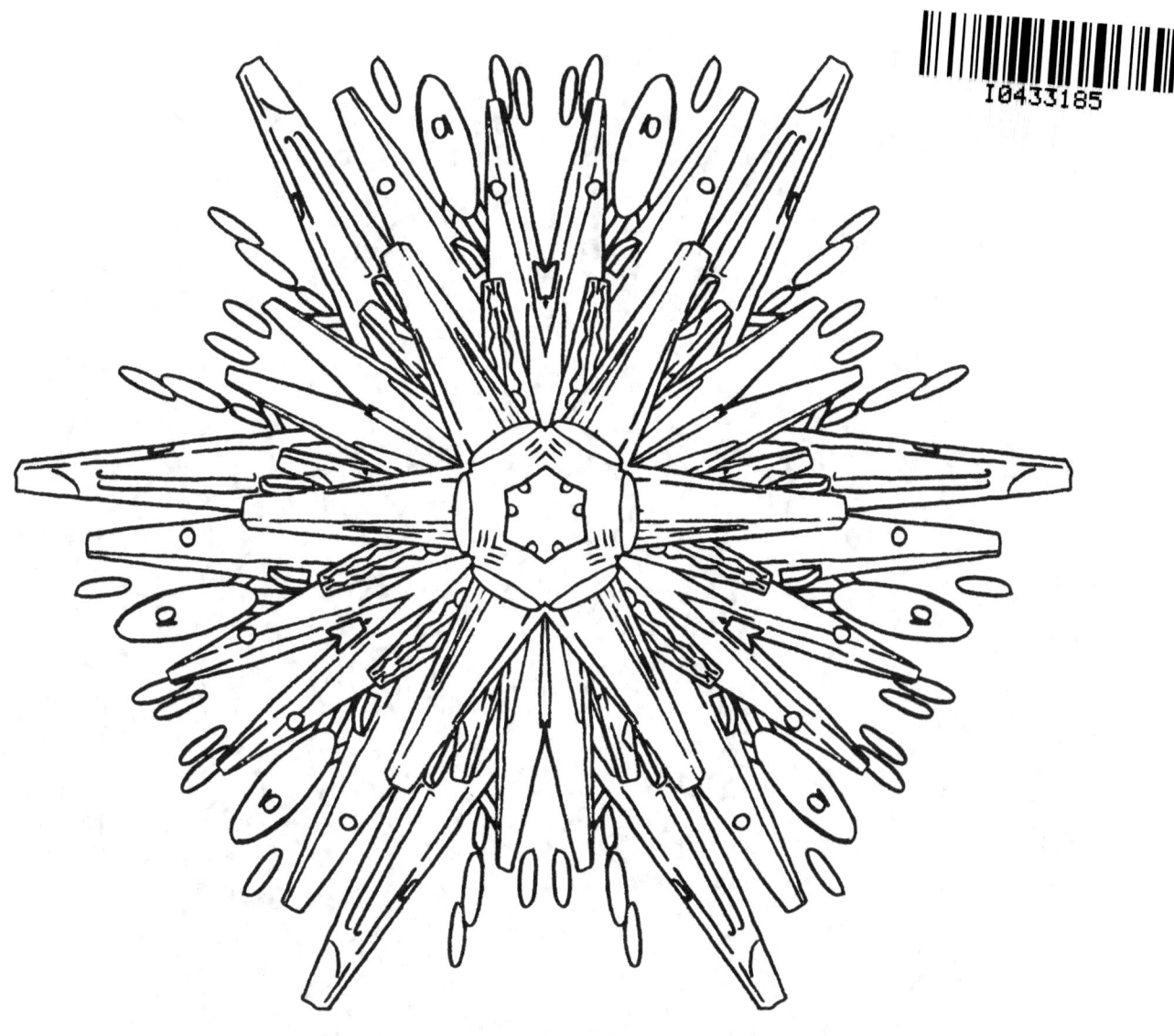

MegaColor
25 Years of Megamurals

The Coloring Book

Meg Saligman Studio

MegaColor Volume One

©2017 MLS Studios LLC

www.megsaligman.com

All rights reserved. No part of this book may be reproduced or transmitted by any form or by any means, electronic or mechanical, including photocopy, recording, or any information storage or retrieval system without prior written consent from the author.

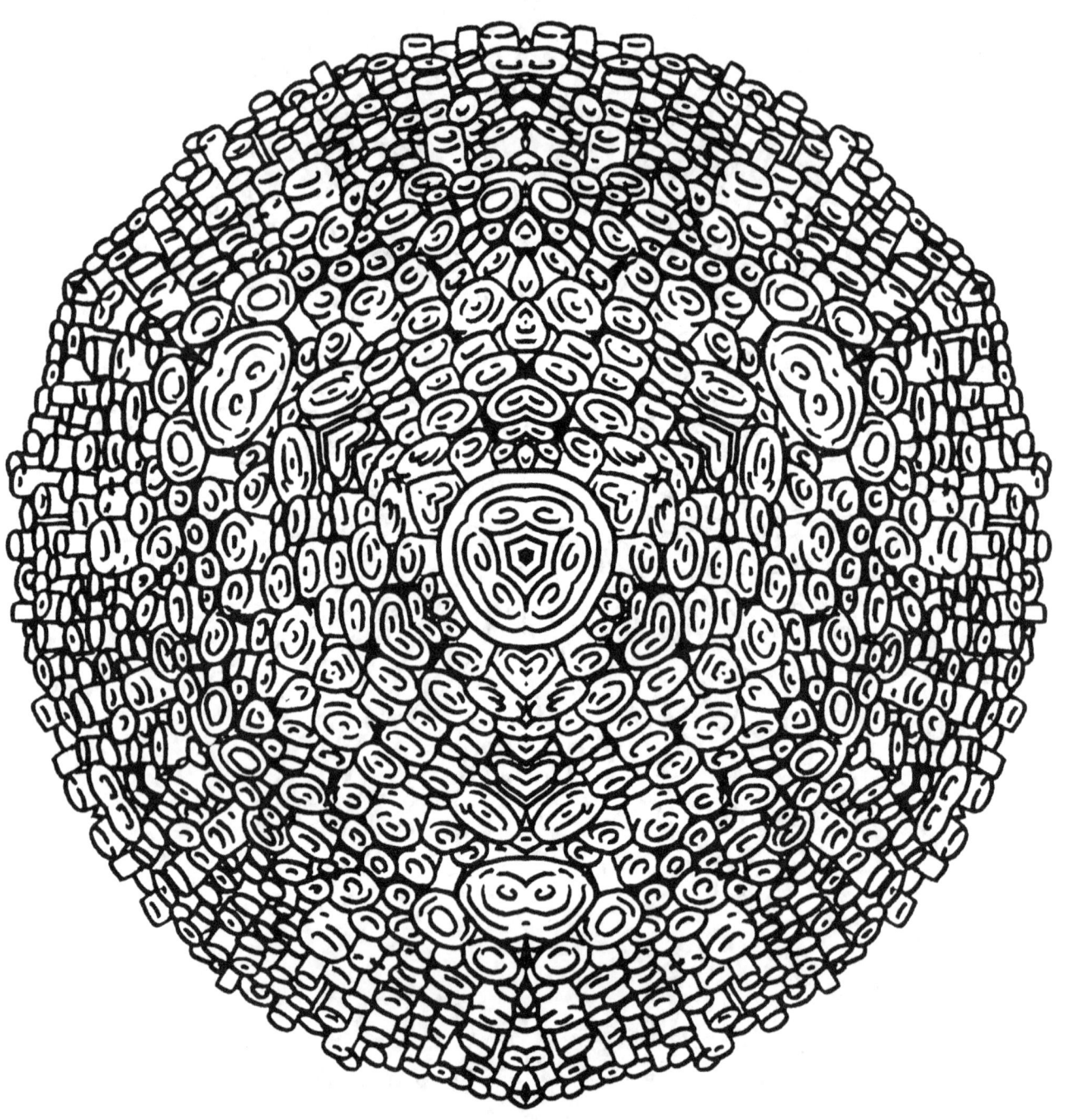

Deep meaning exists for me when people come together
and create something purposeful and beautiful with their hands.
As a public artist who loves collaboration,

I invite you to
come create with me
and color our world.
—Meg

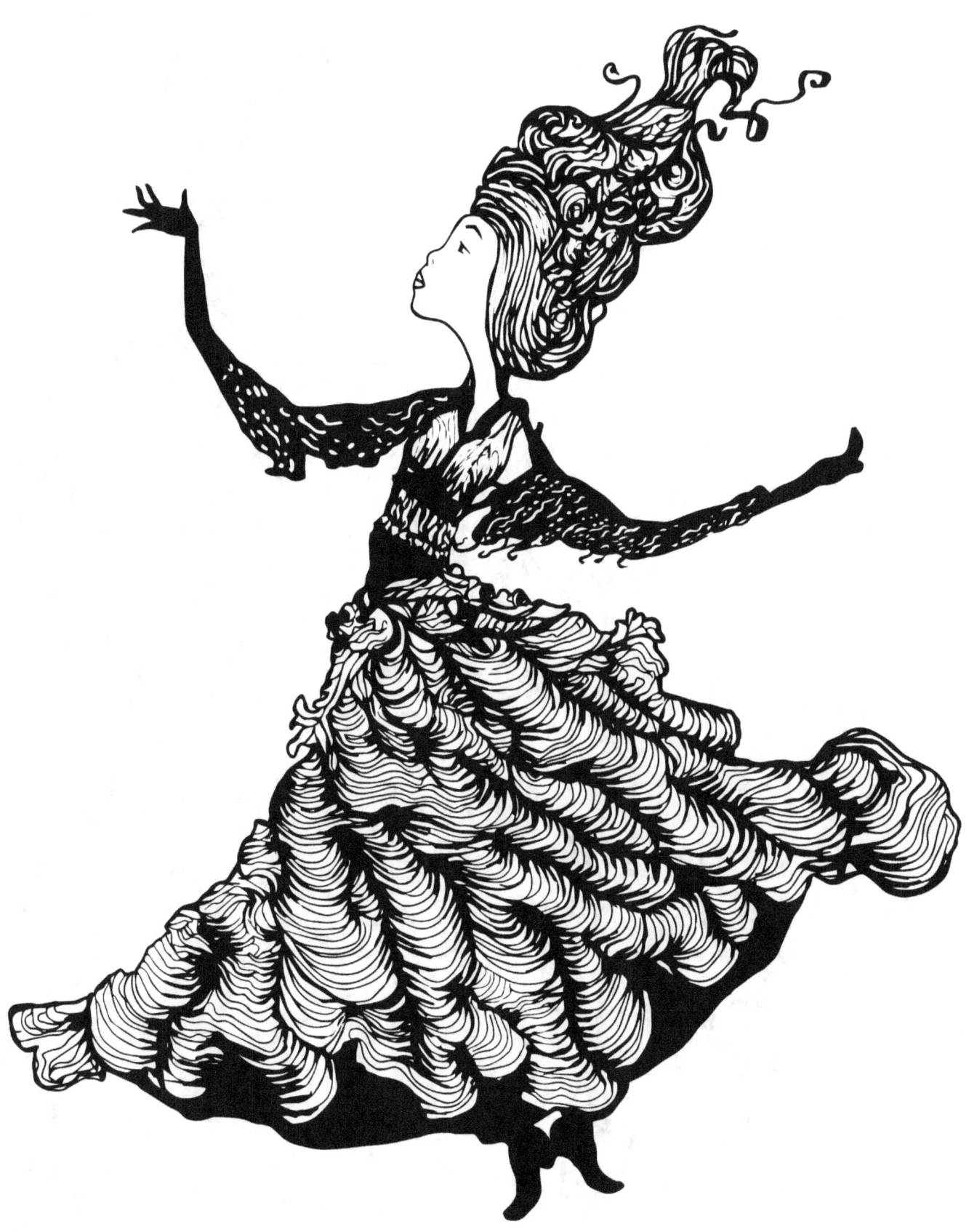

Rules? No rules.

Empty Space? Have at it!

Show every page in this book who's boss.

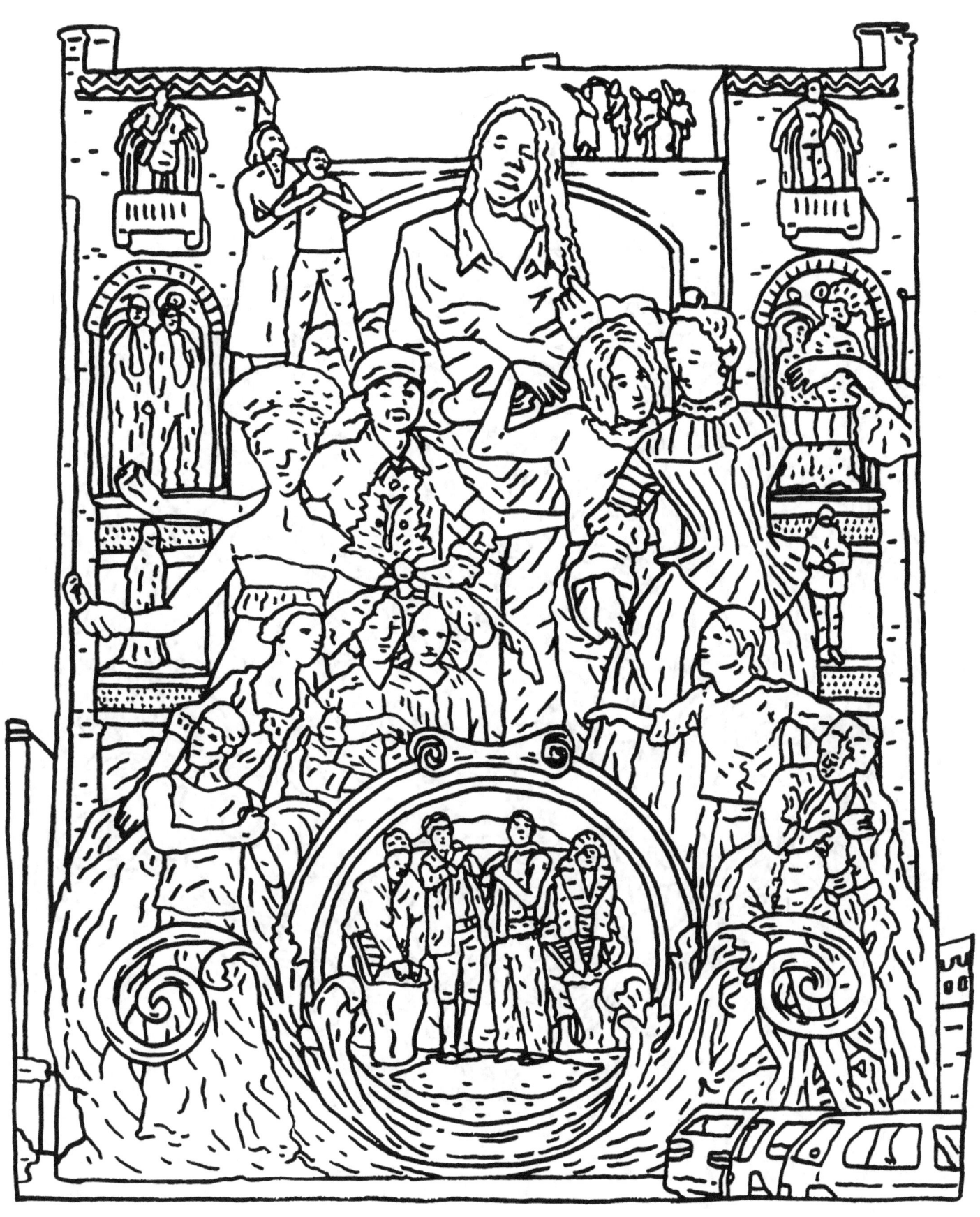

The "Mona Lisa of Broad Street" shows the power of drawing outside the lines... so can you!

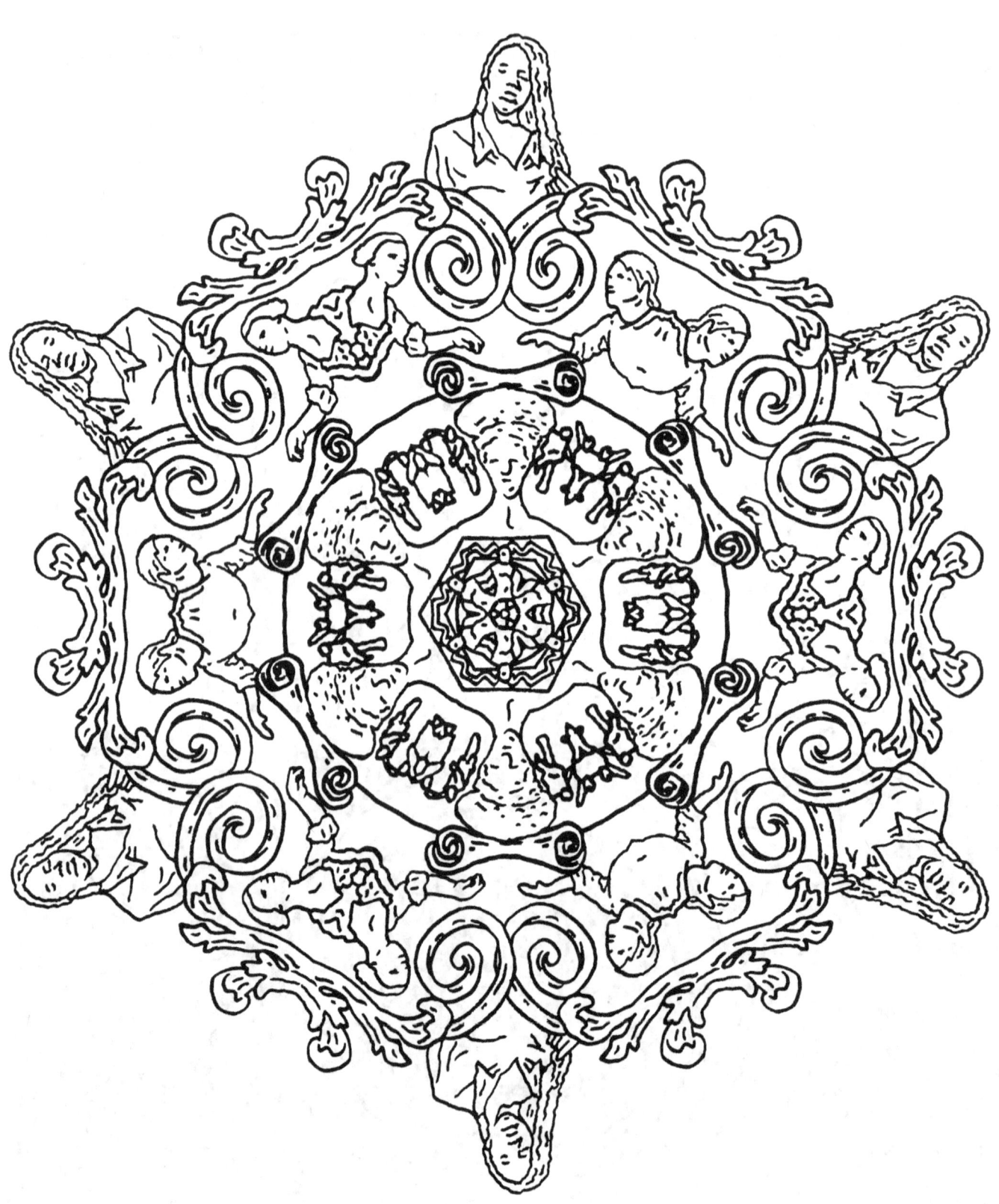

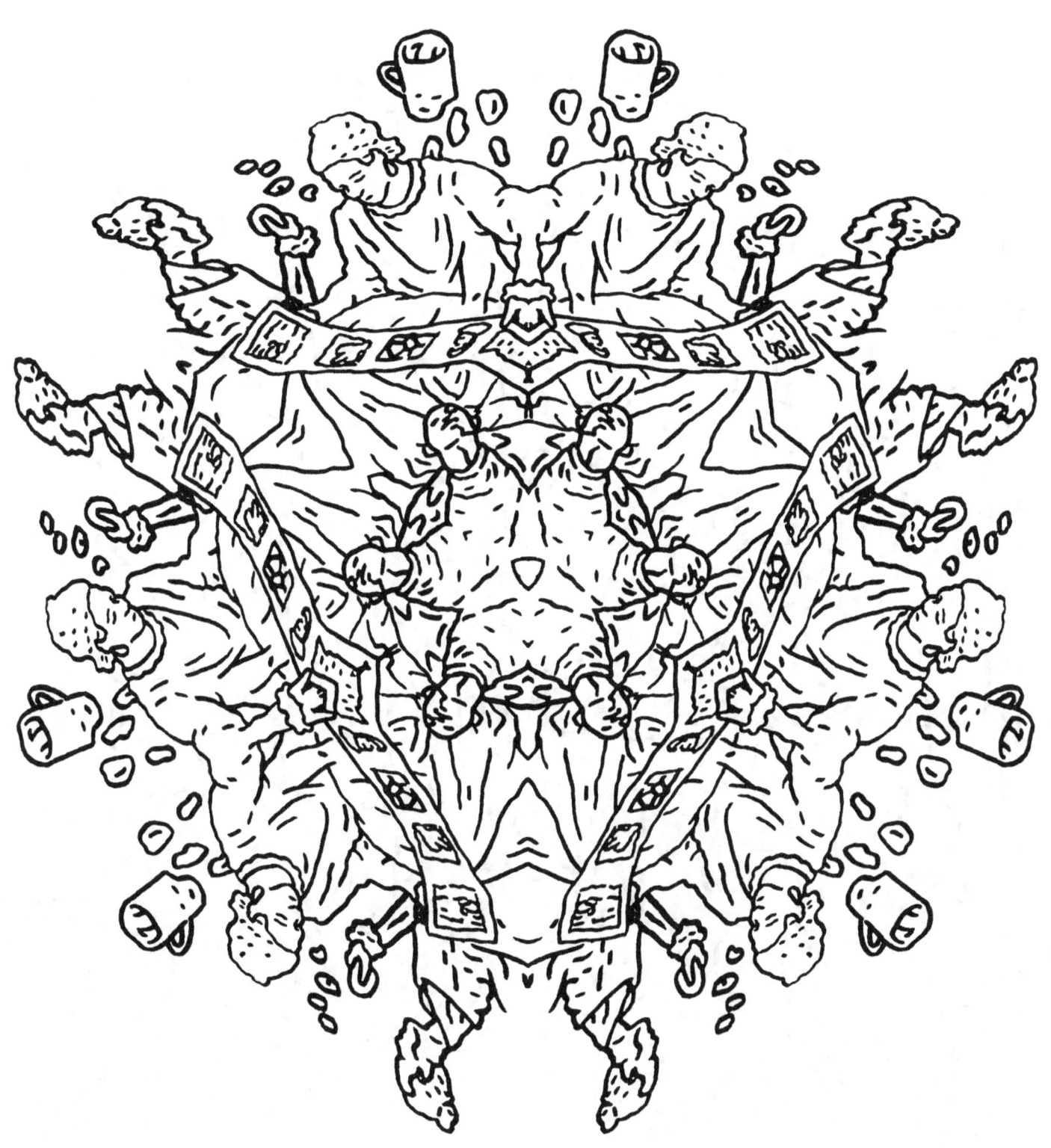

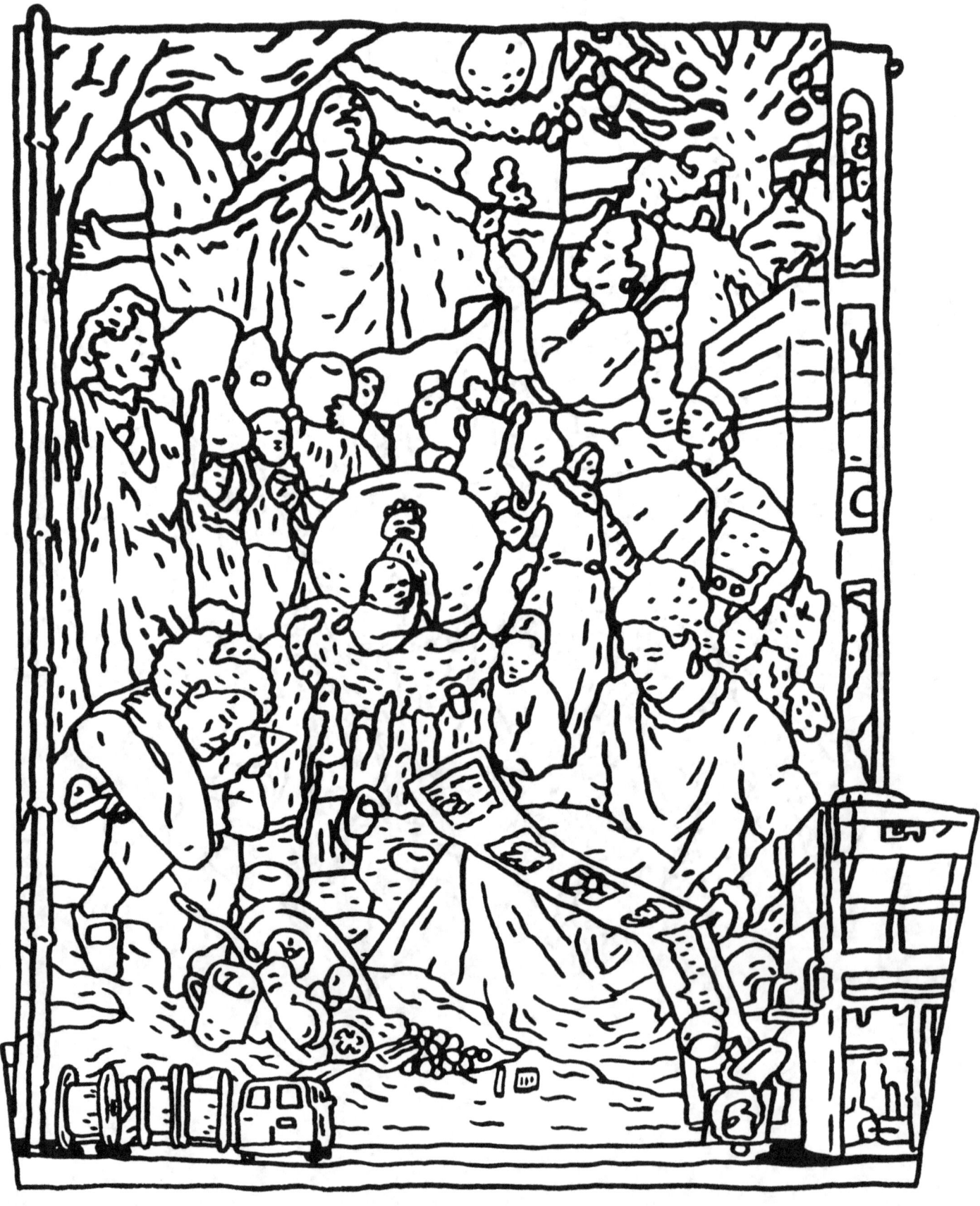

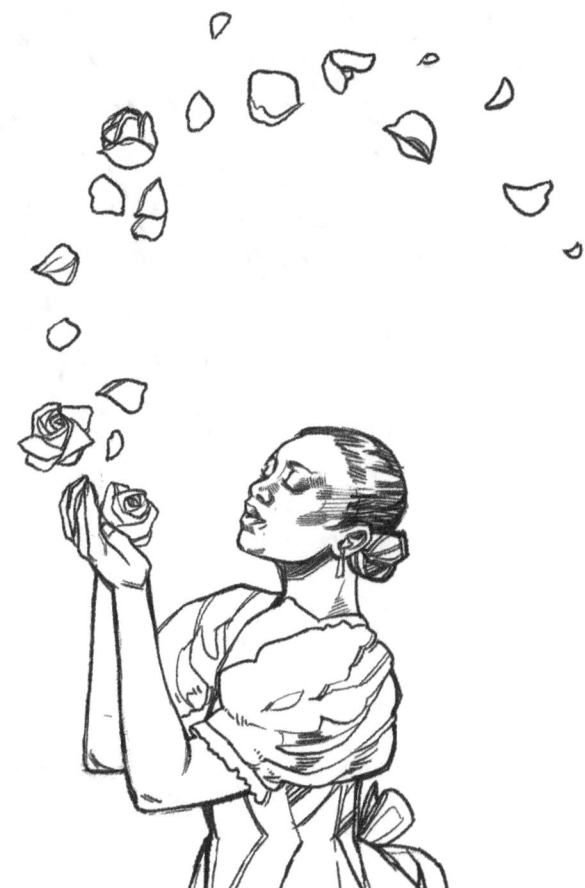

Over 2,000 community members worked on this mural in celebration of the second millennium. Join them in making up your own Millennium Moon.

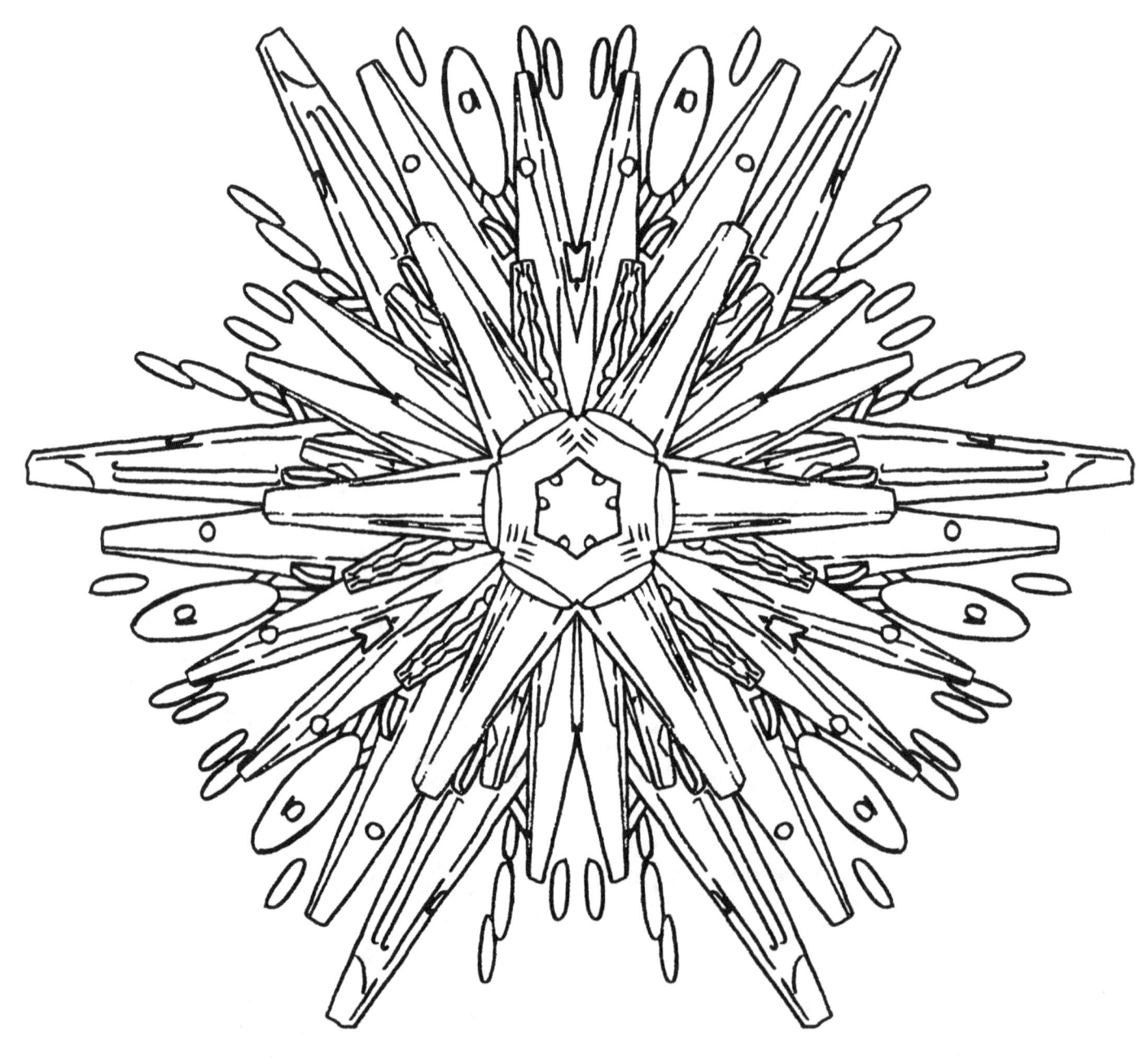

Vote for the Good Life!

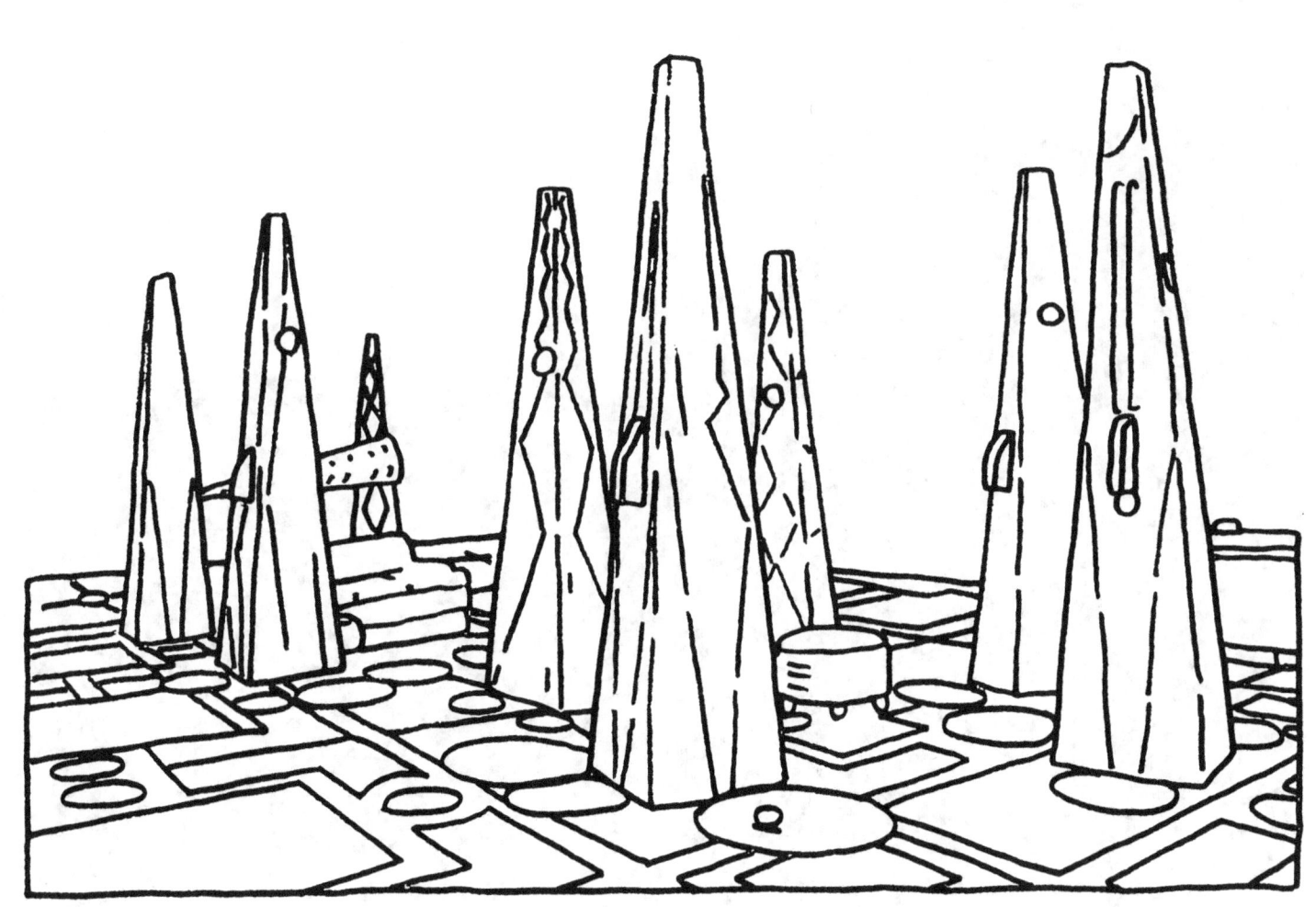

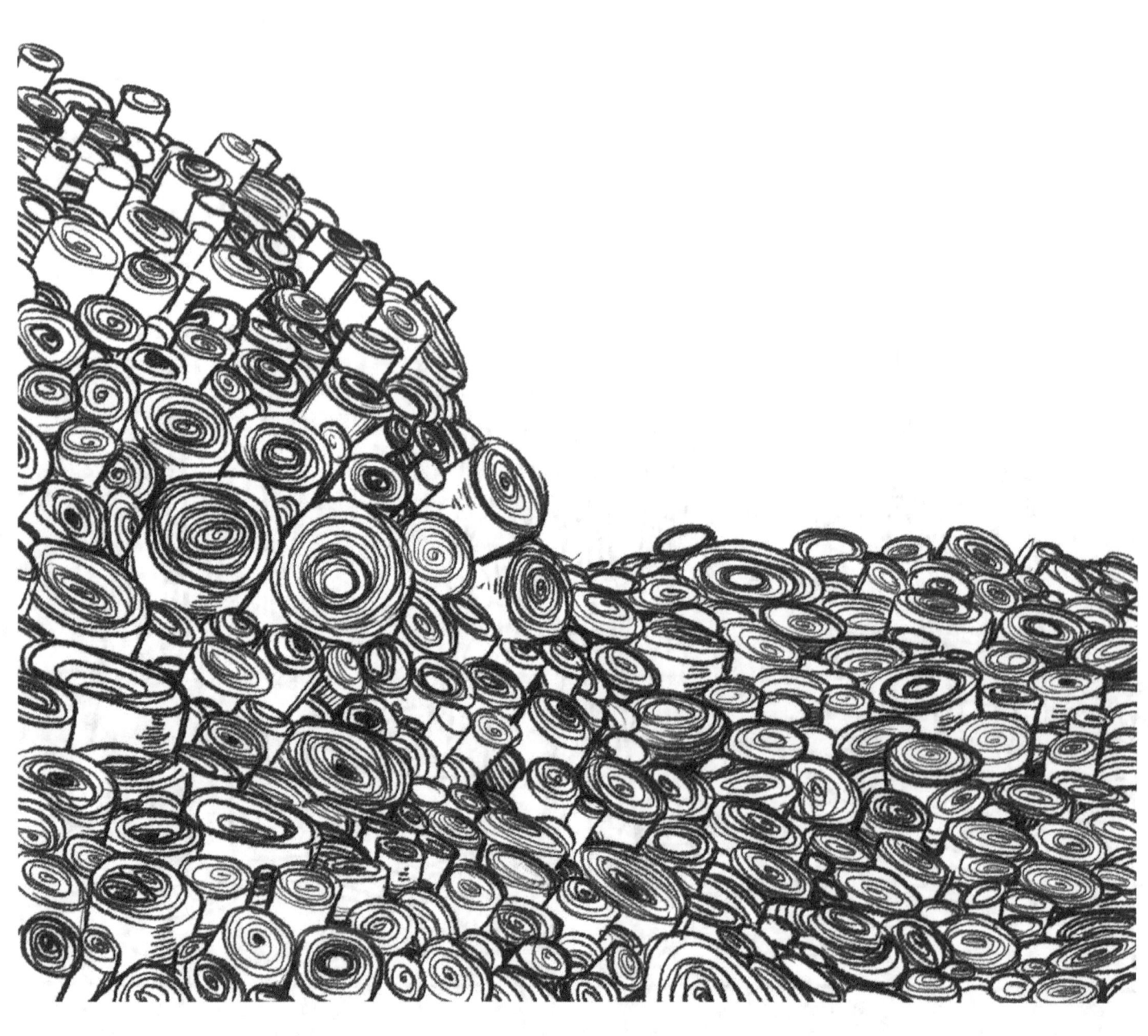

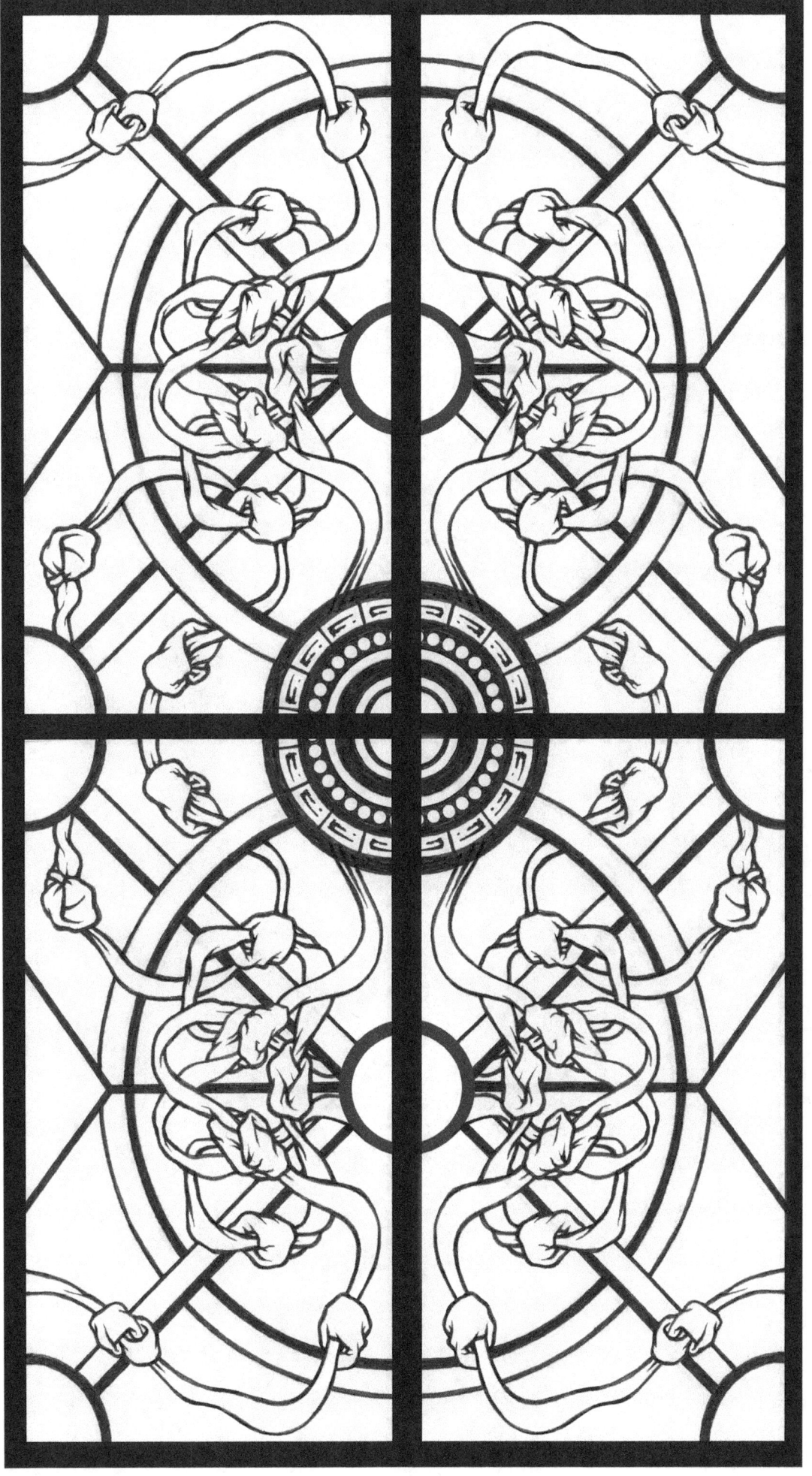

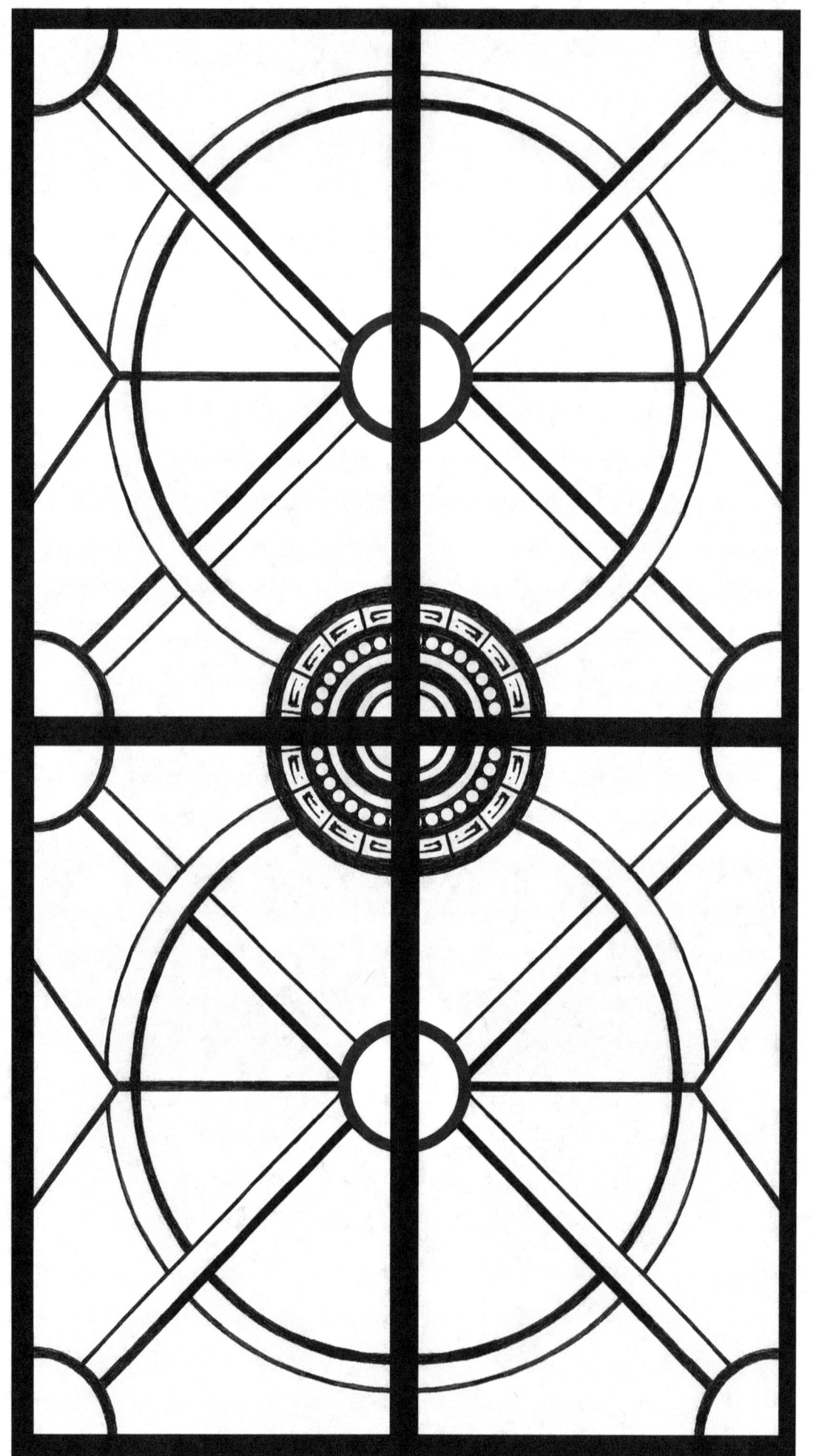

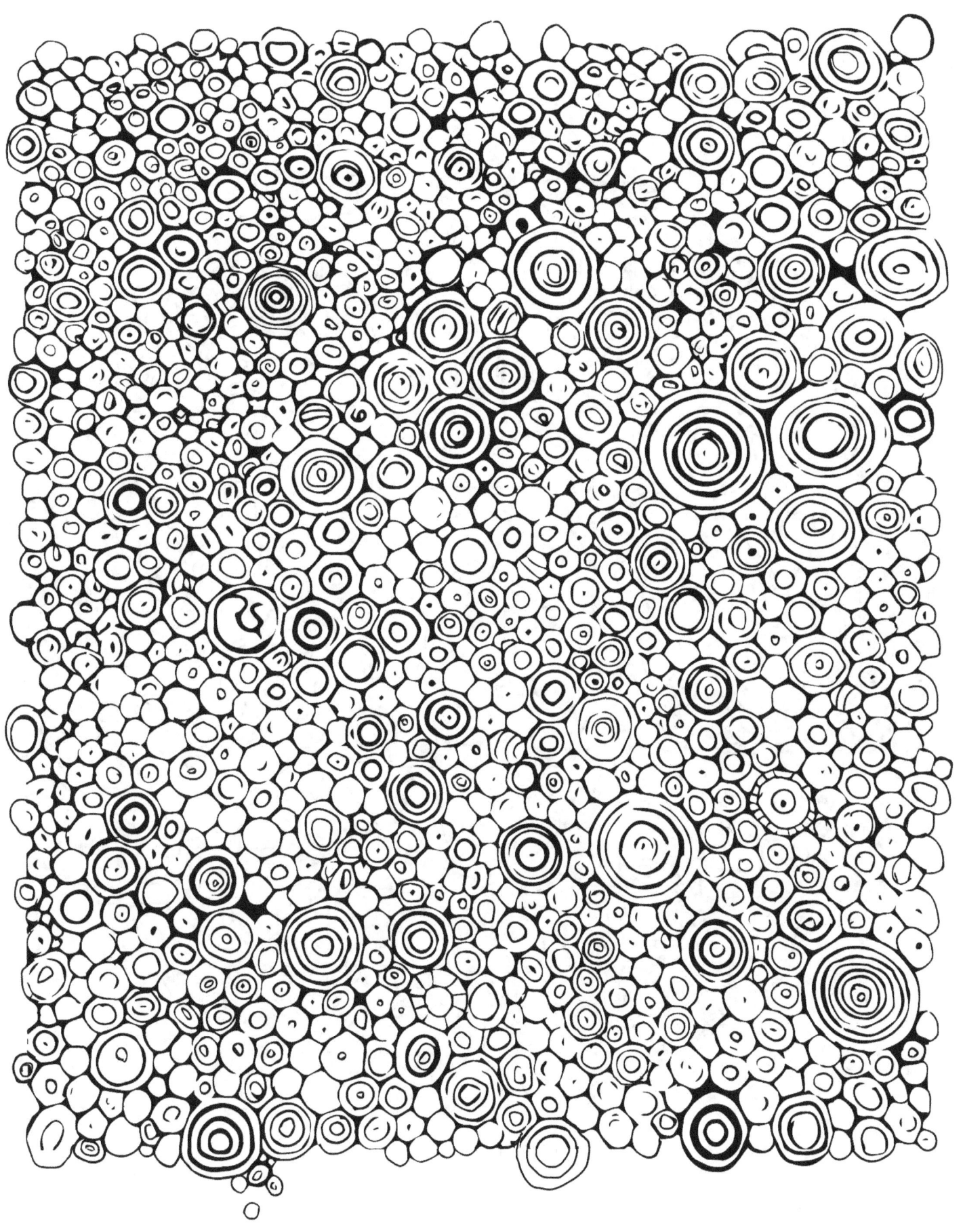

What happens when spiritual energy becomes real? Knot-topia, of course!

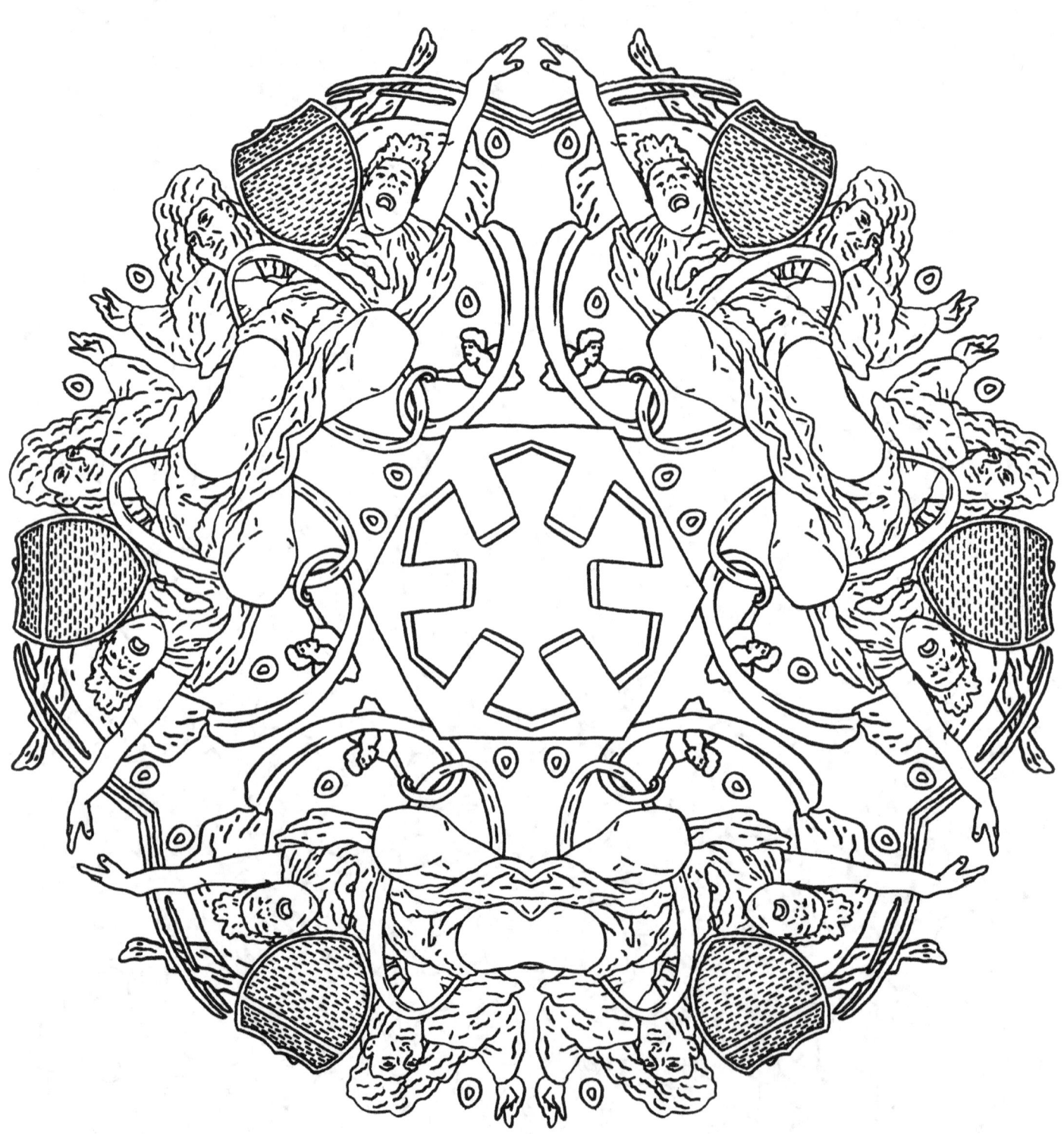

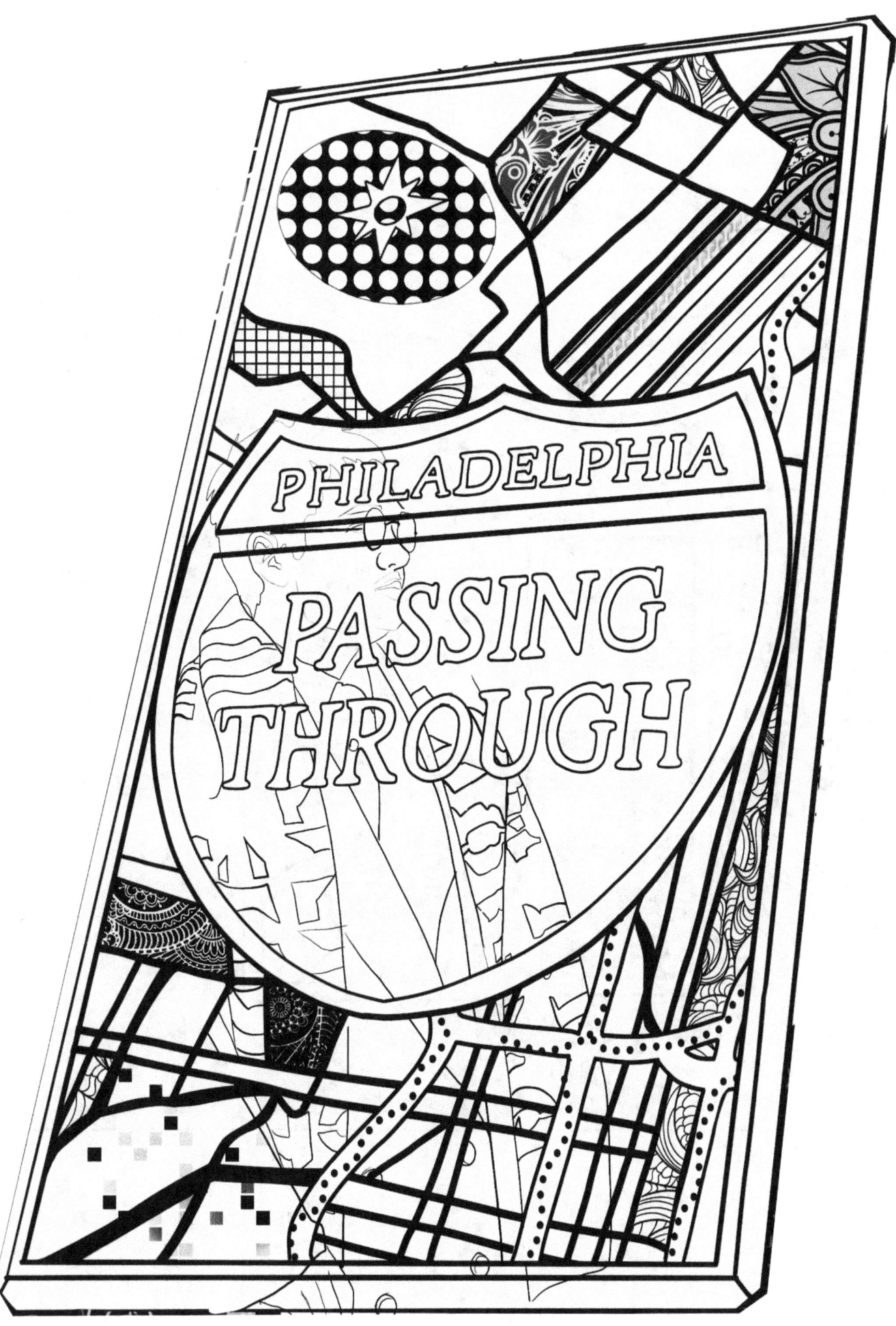

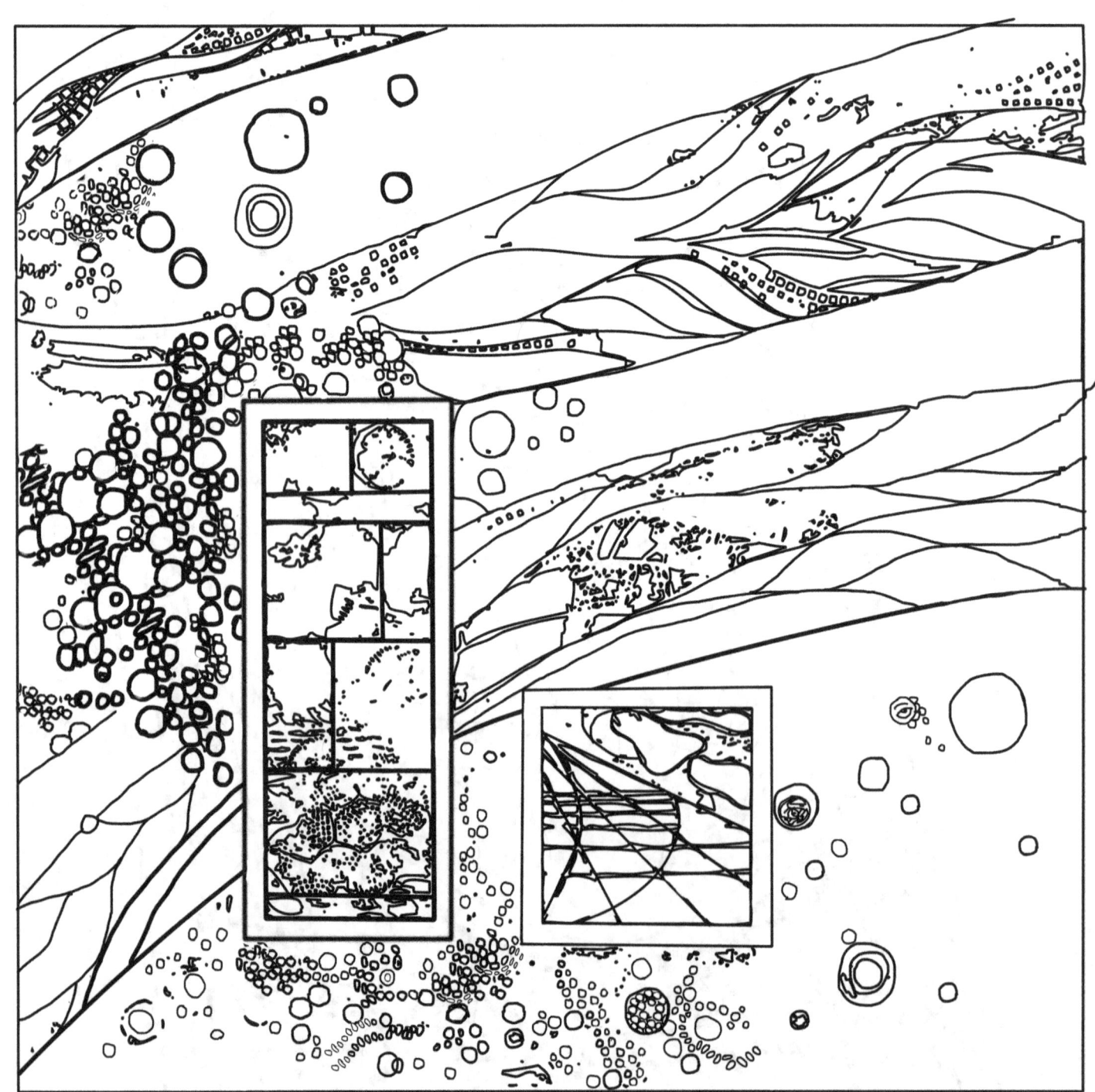

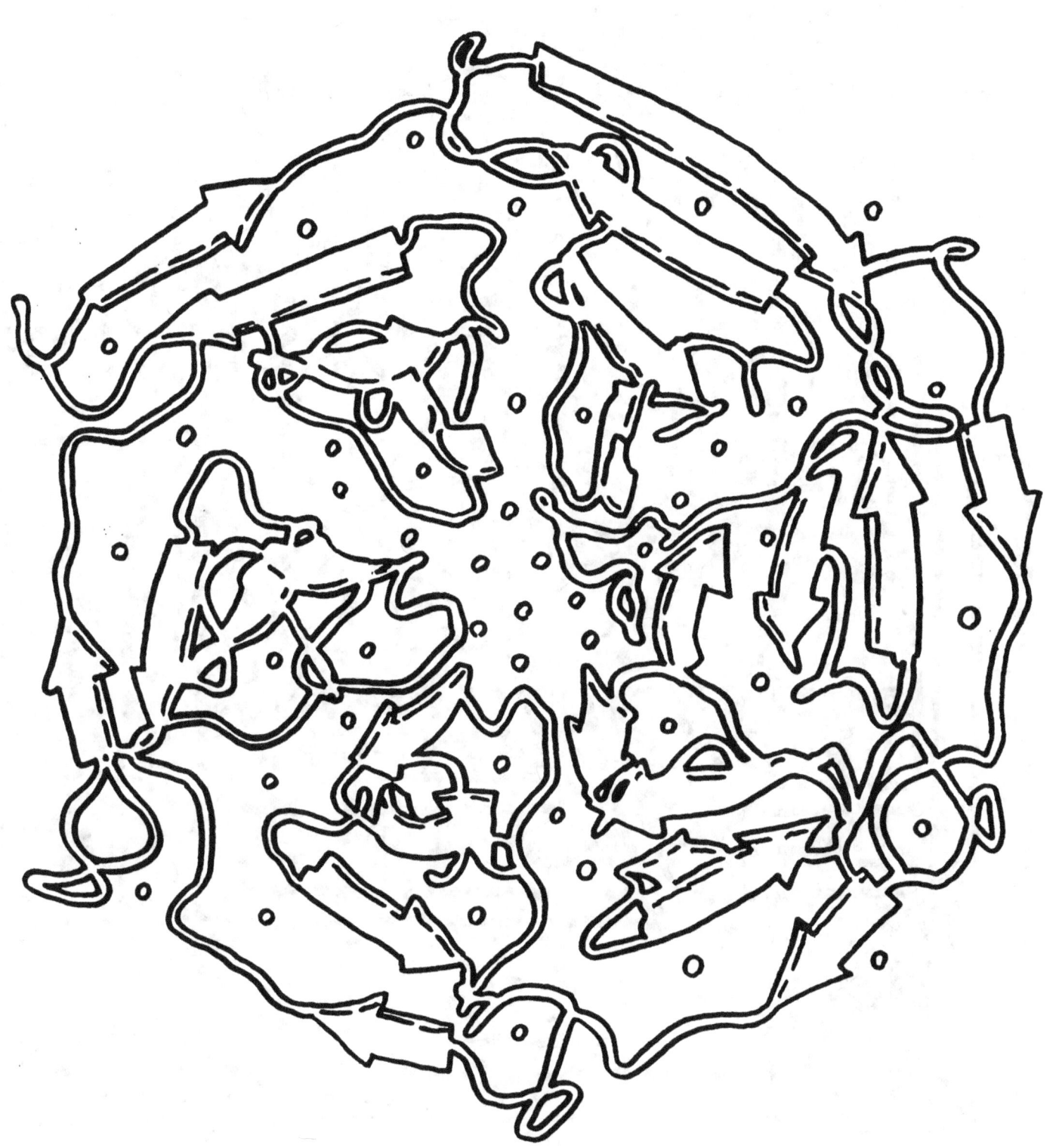

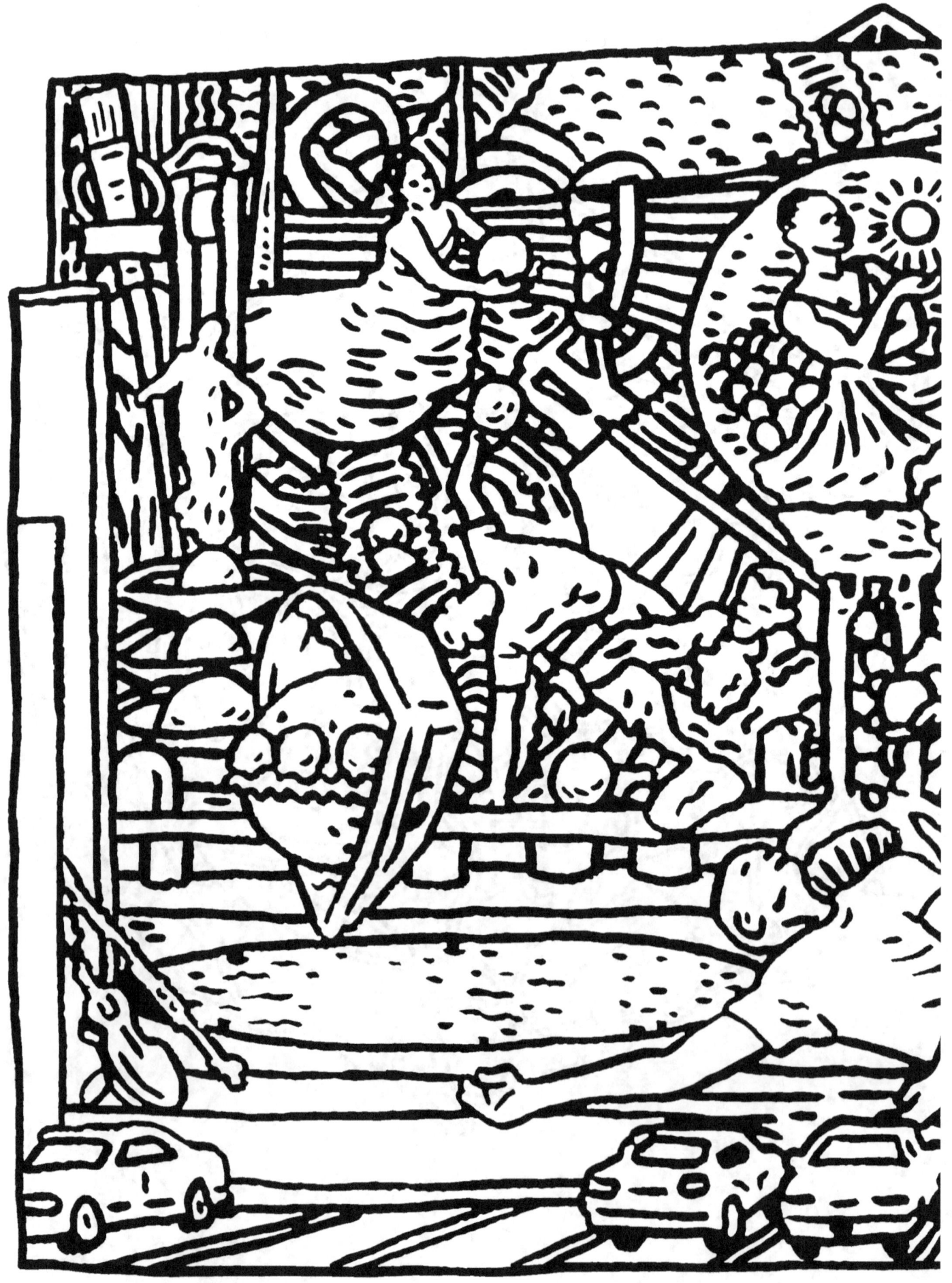

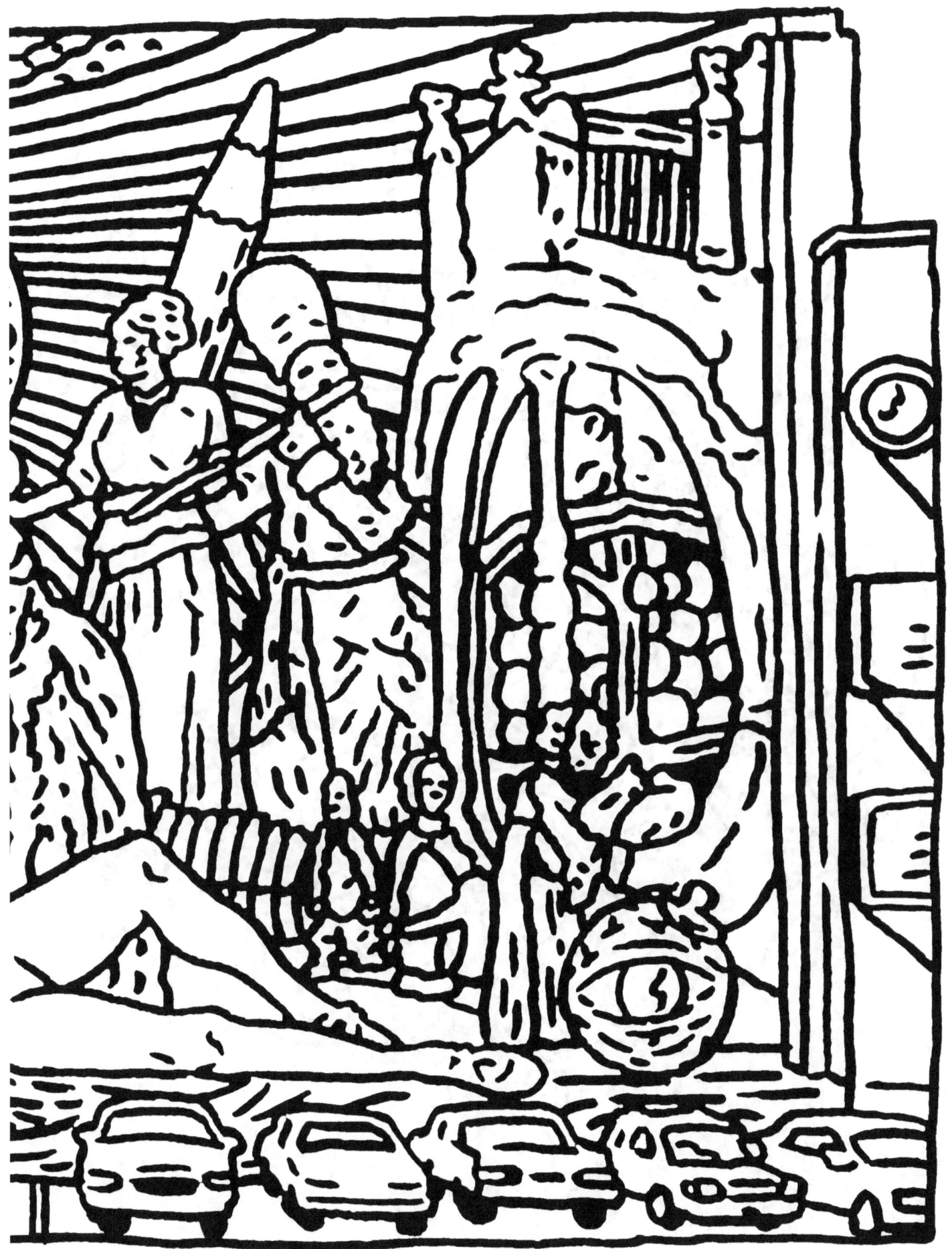

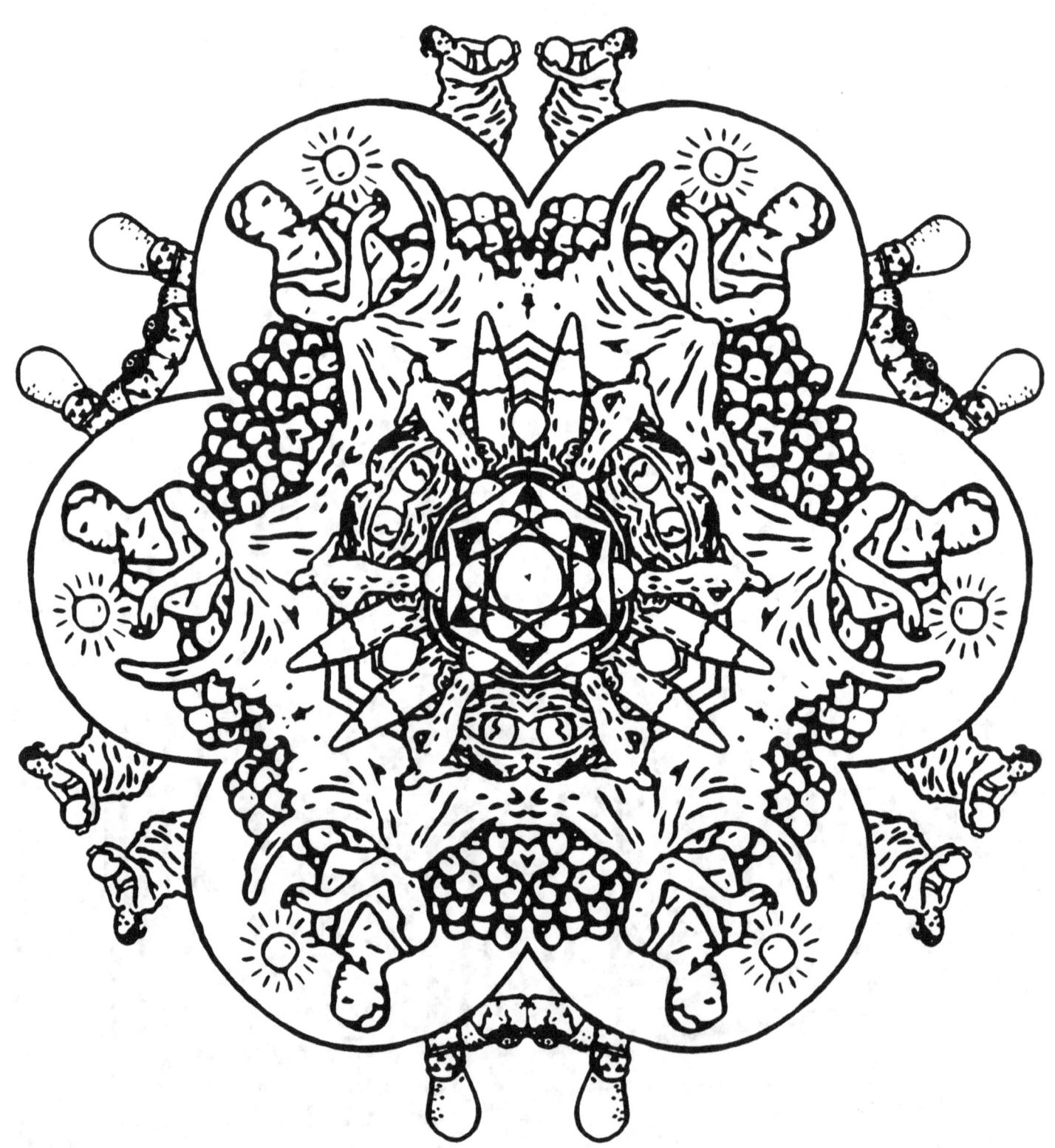

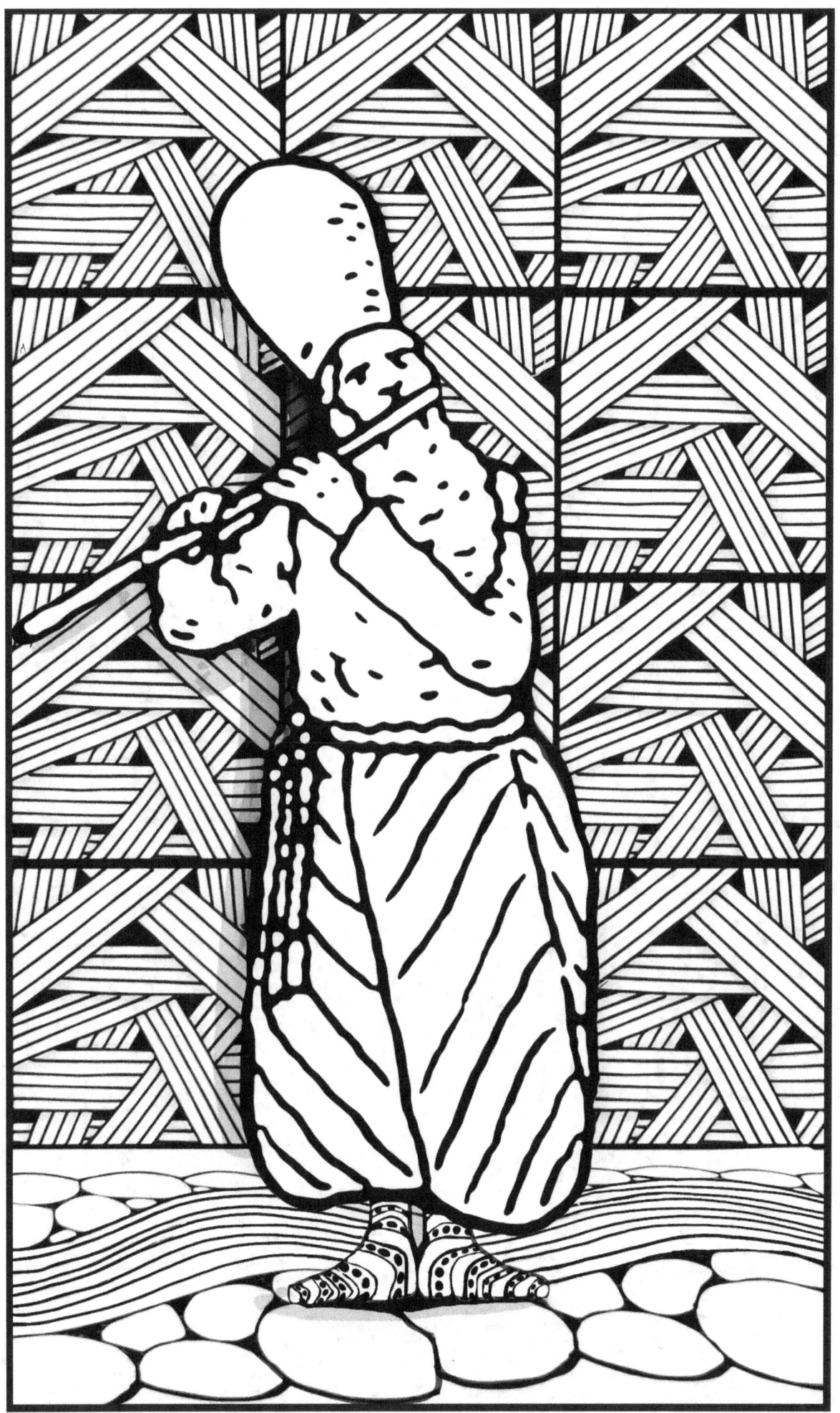

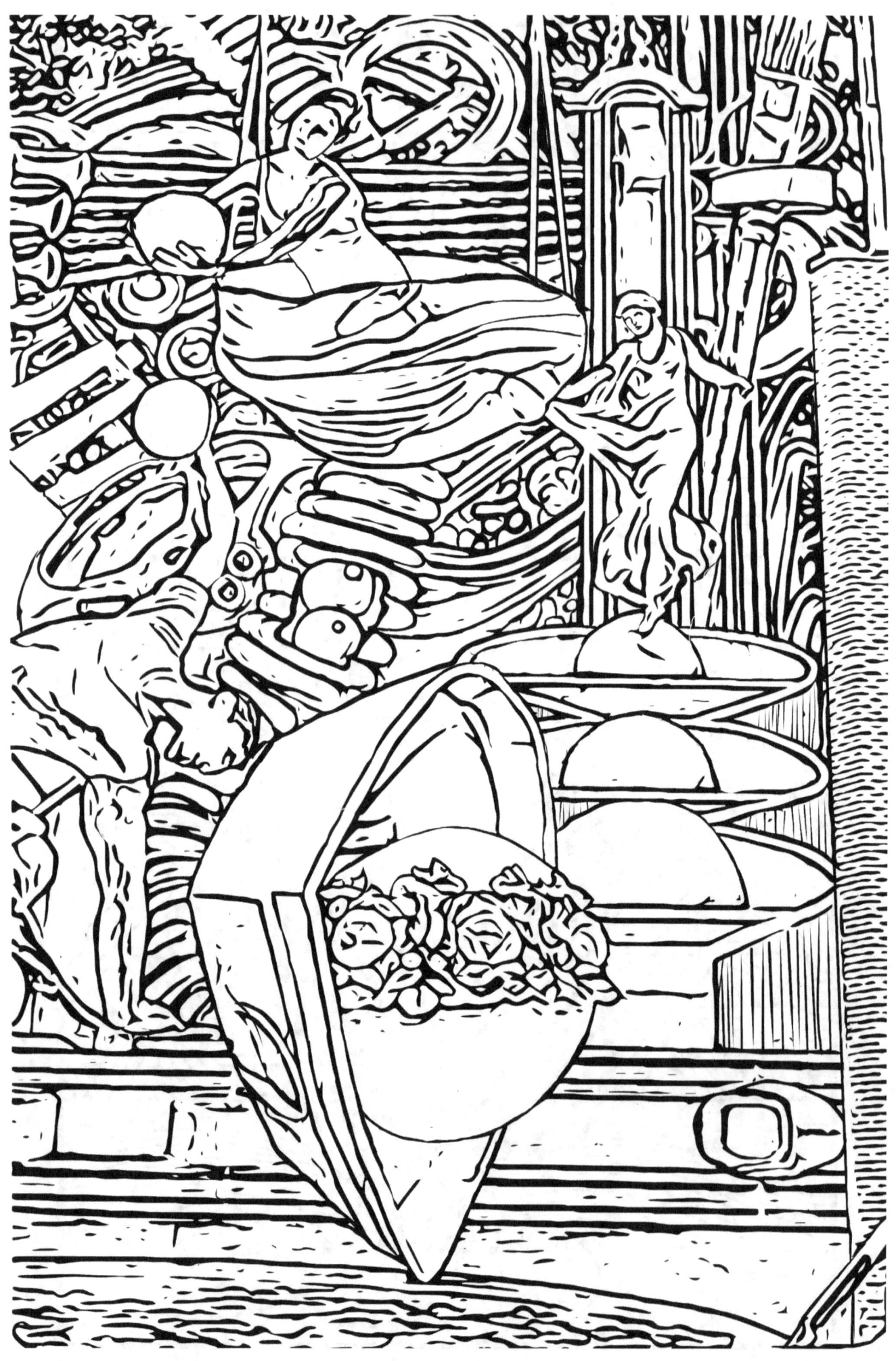

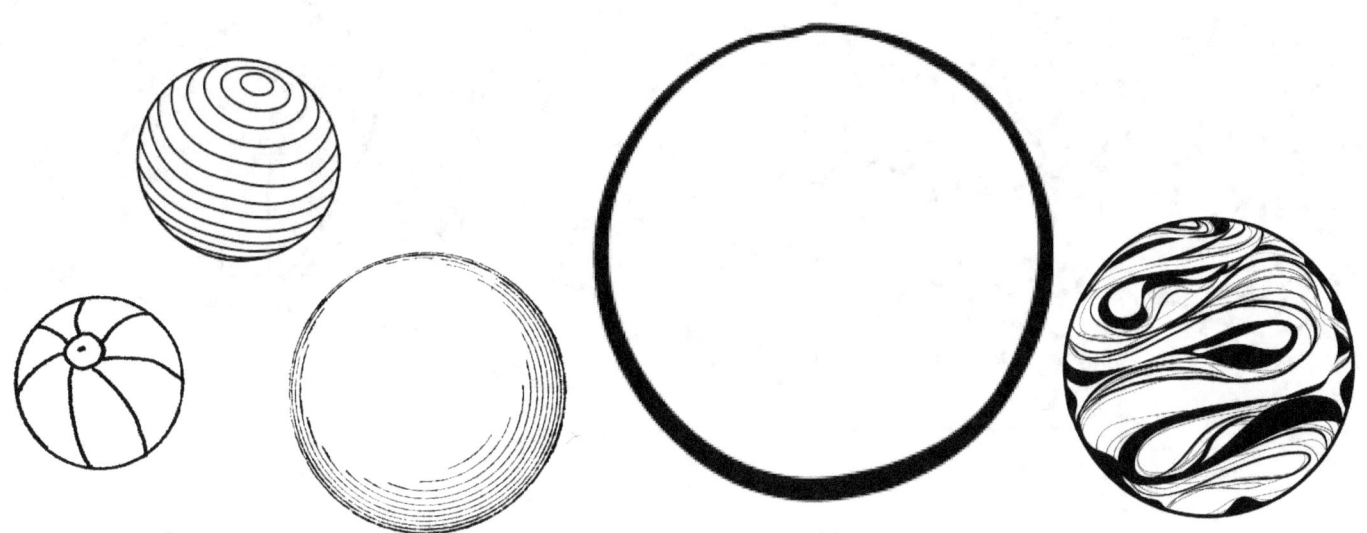

Our Muses have a serious case of the sphere!
It's the perfect art form with no beginning, end, top or bottom.
Round out our collection and design your own.

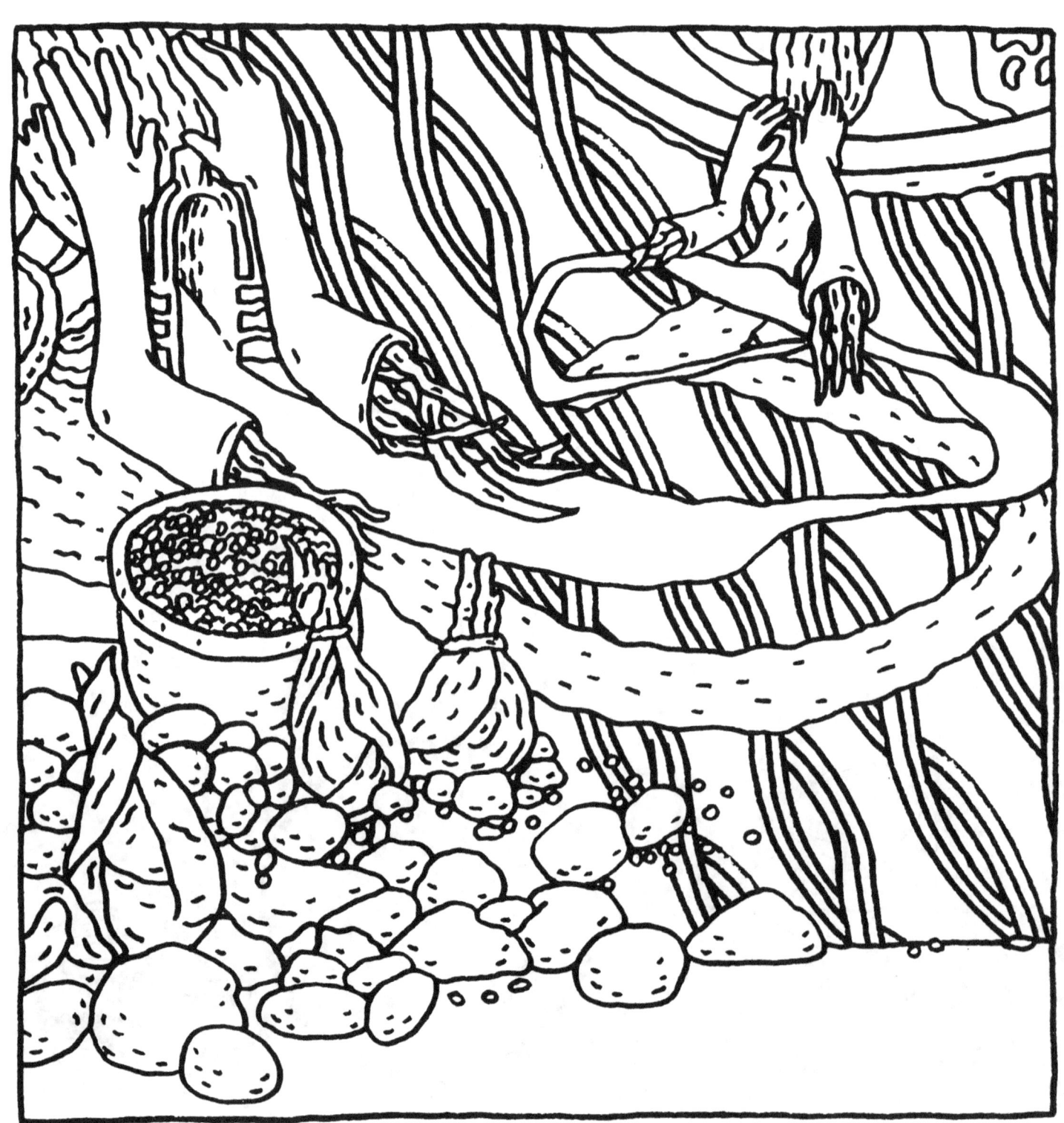

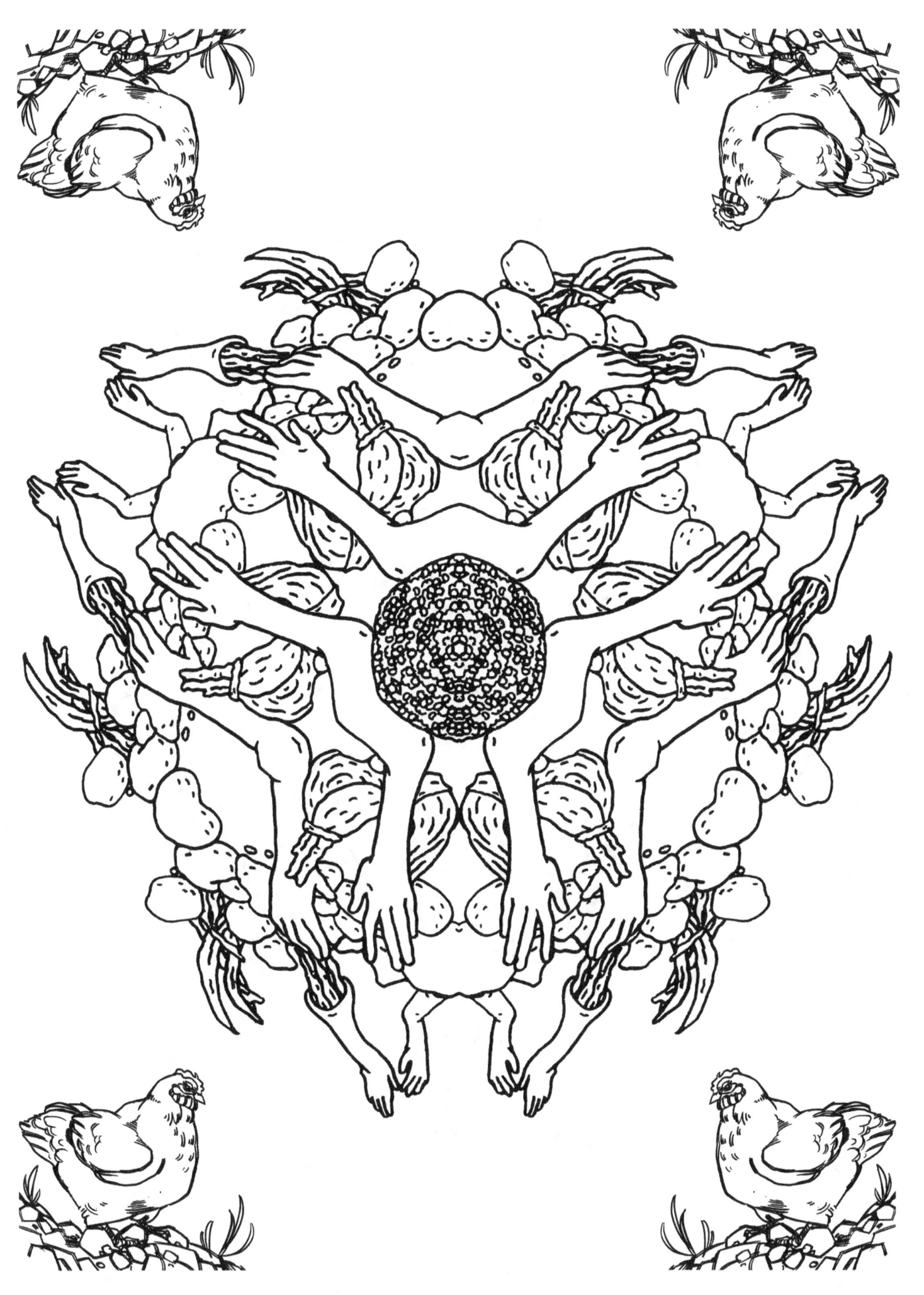

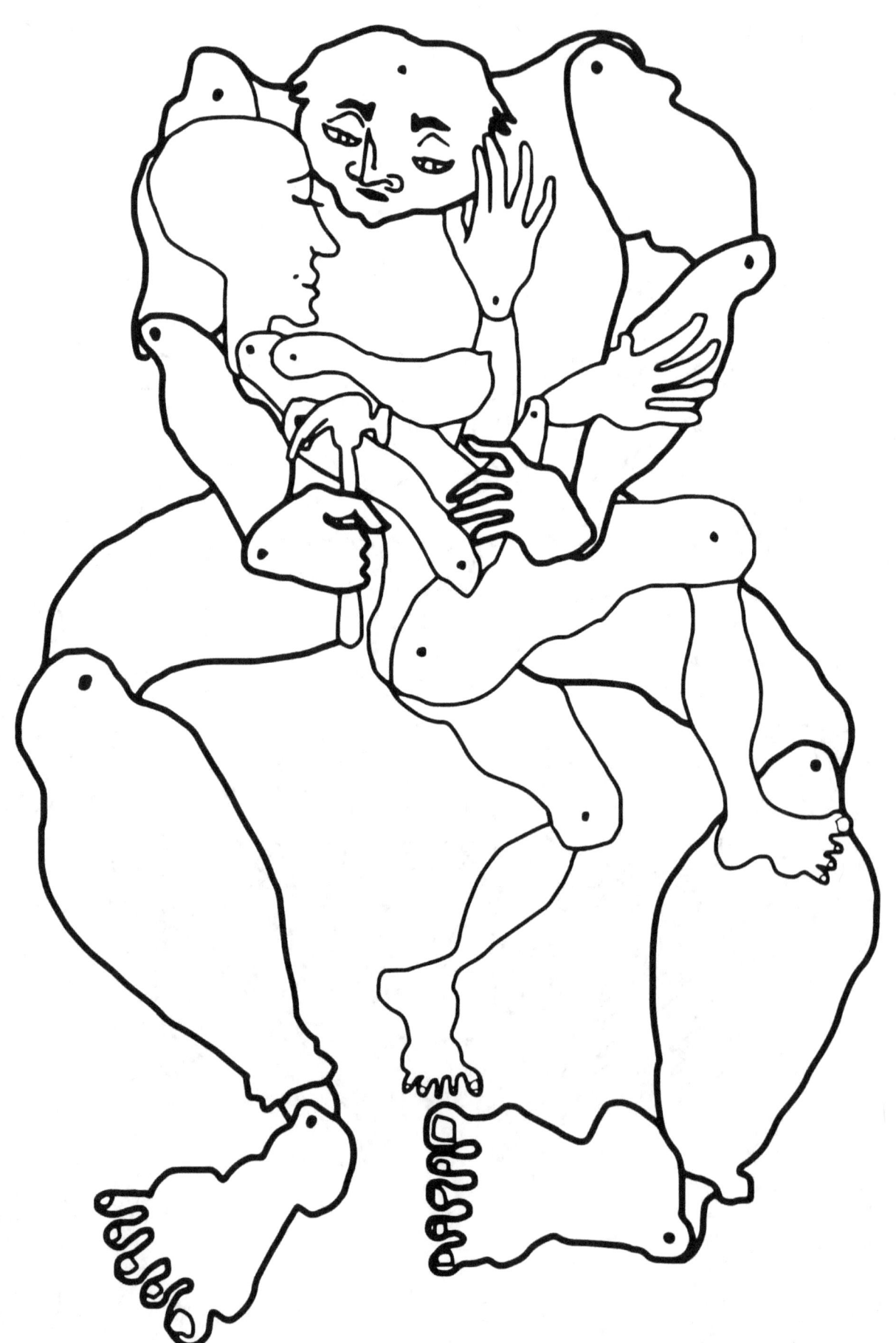

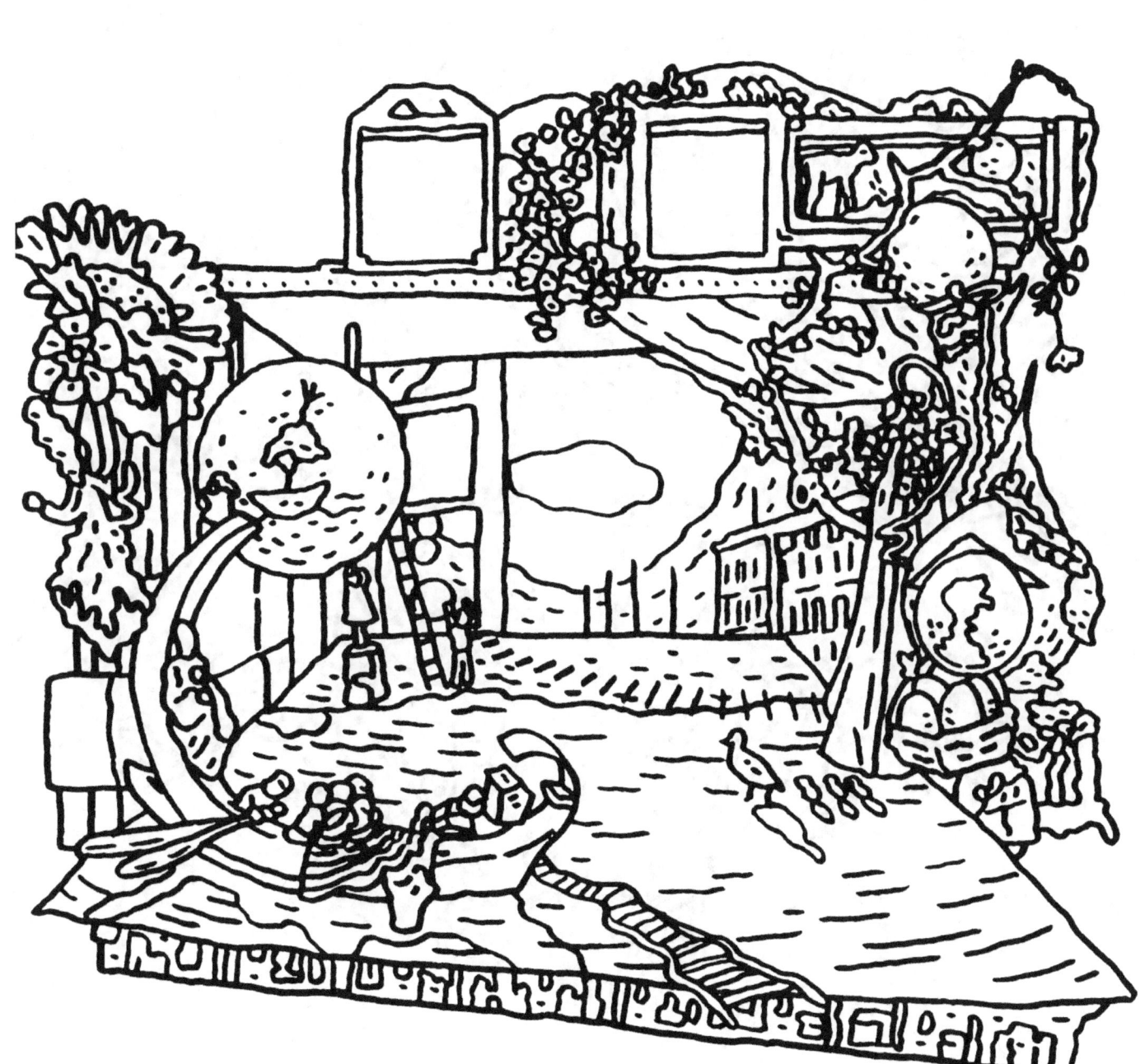

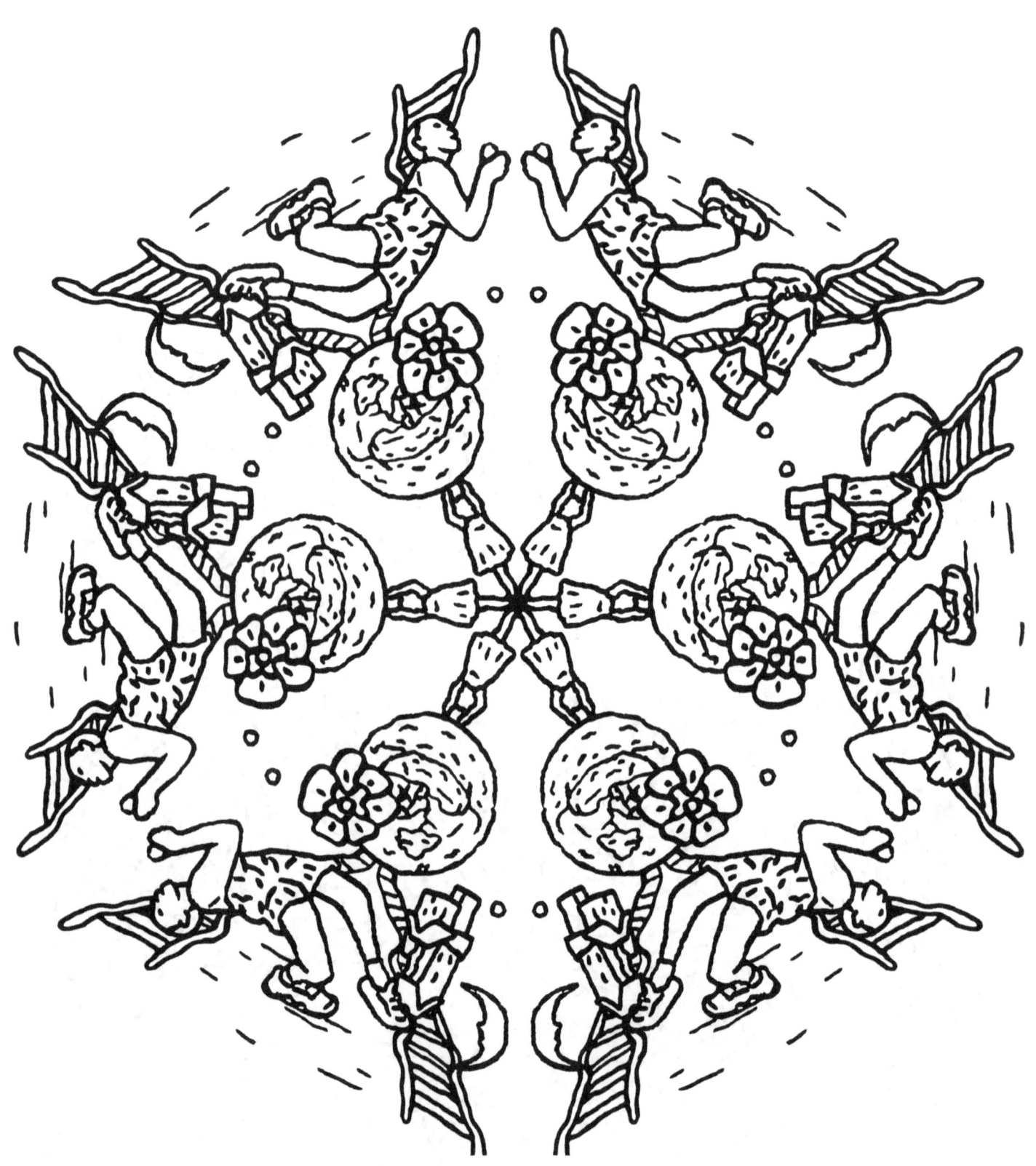

Pictures from words, words from pictures.
How about yours?

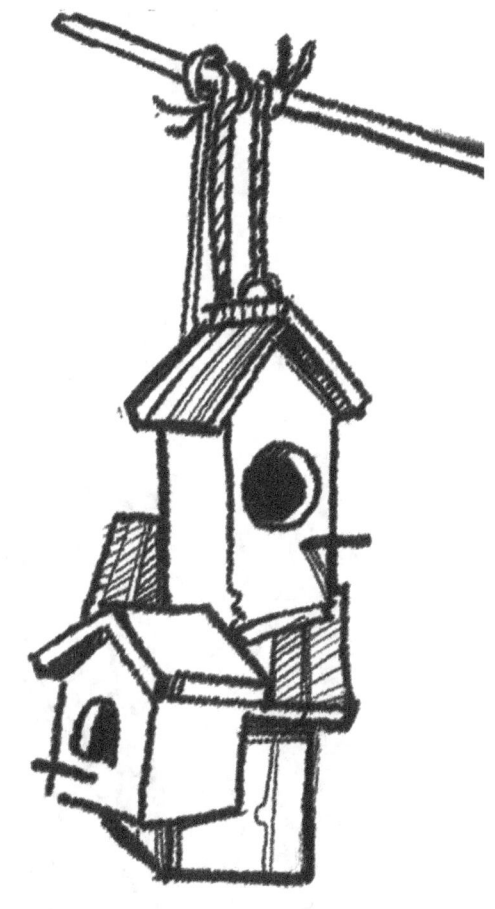

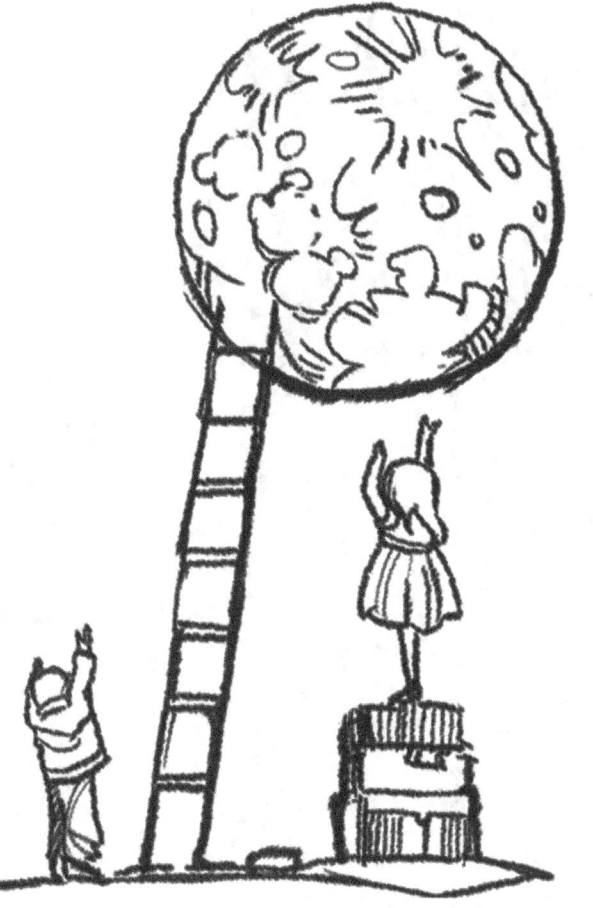

It's only a paper moon,
hanging over a cardboard sea,
but it wouldn't be make believe
if you believed in me.

excerpted lyrics from the song, "It's Only a Paper Moon"
written by E.Y. Harburg and Billy Rose (1933)

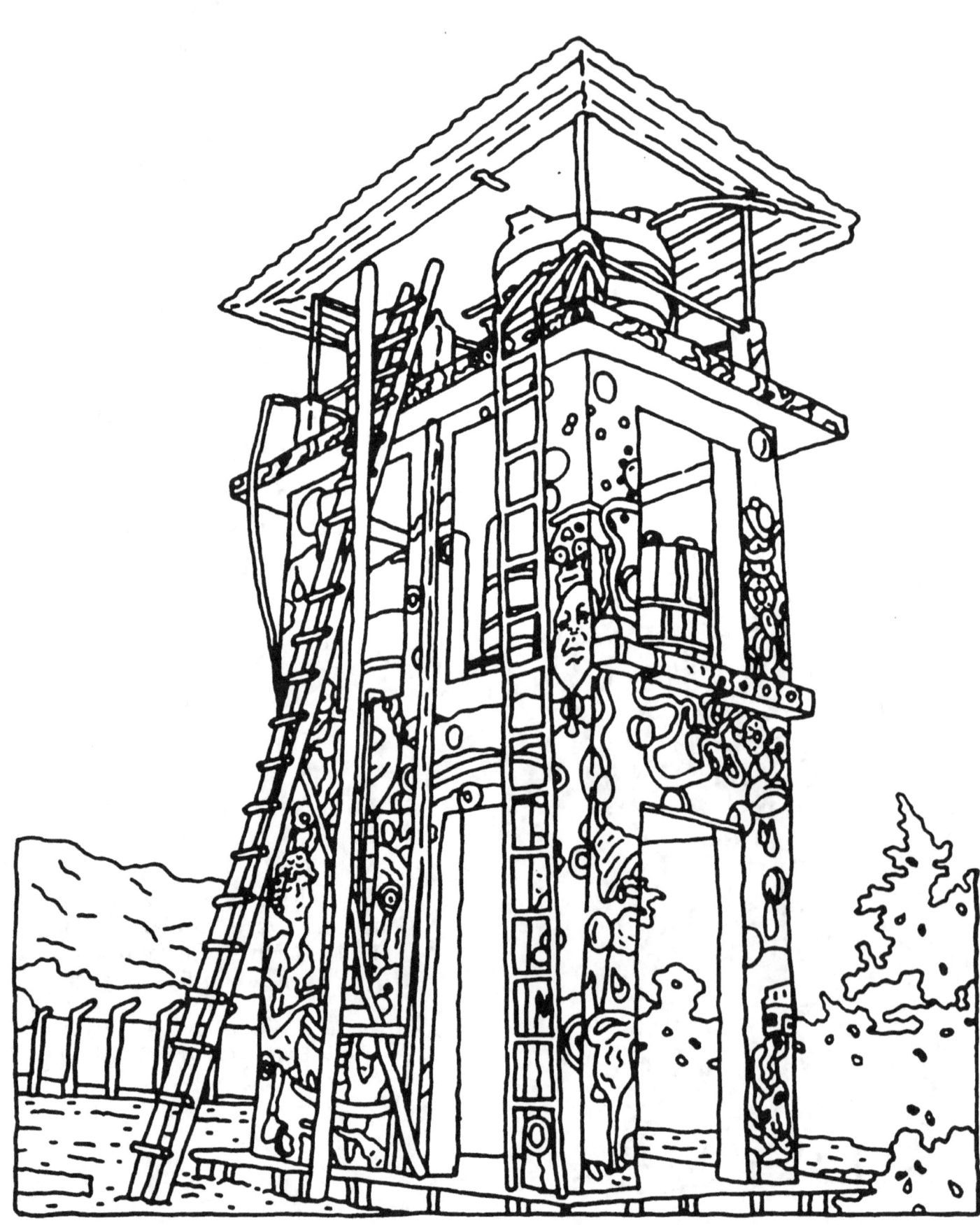

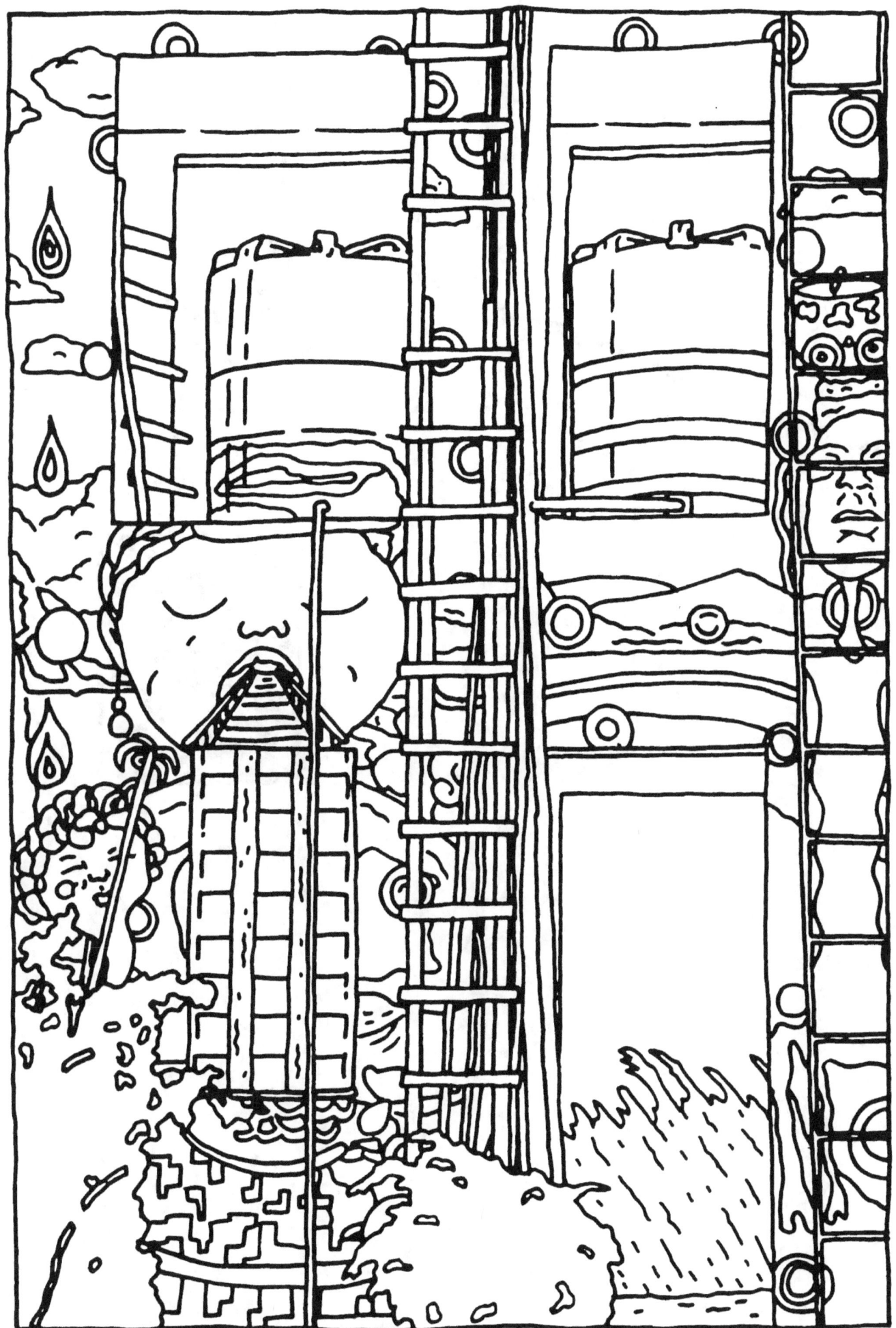

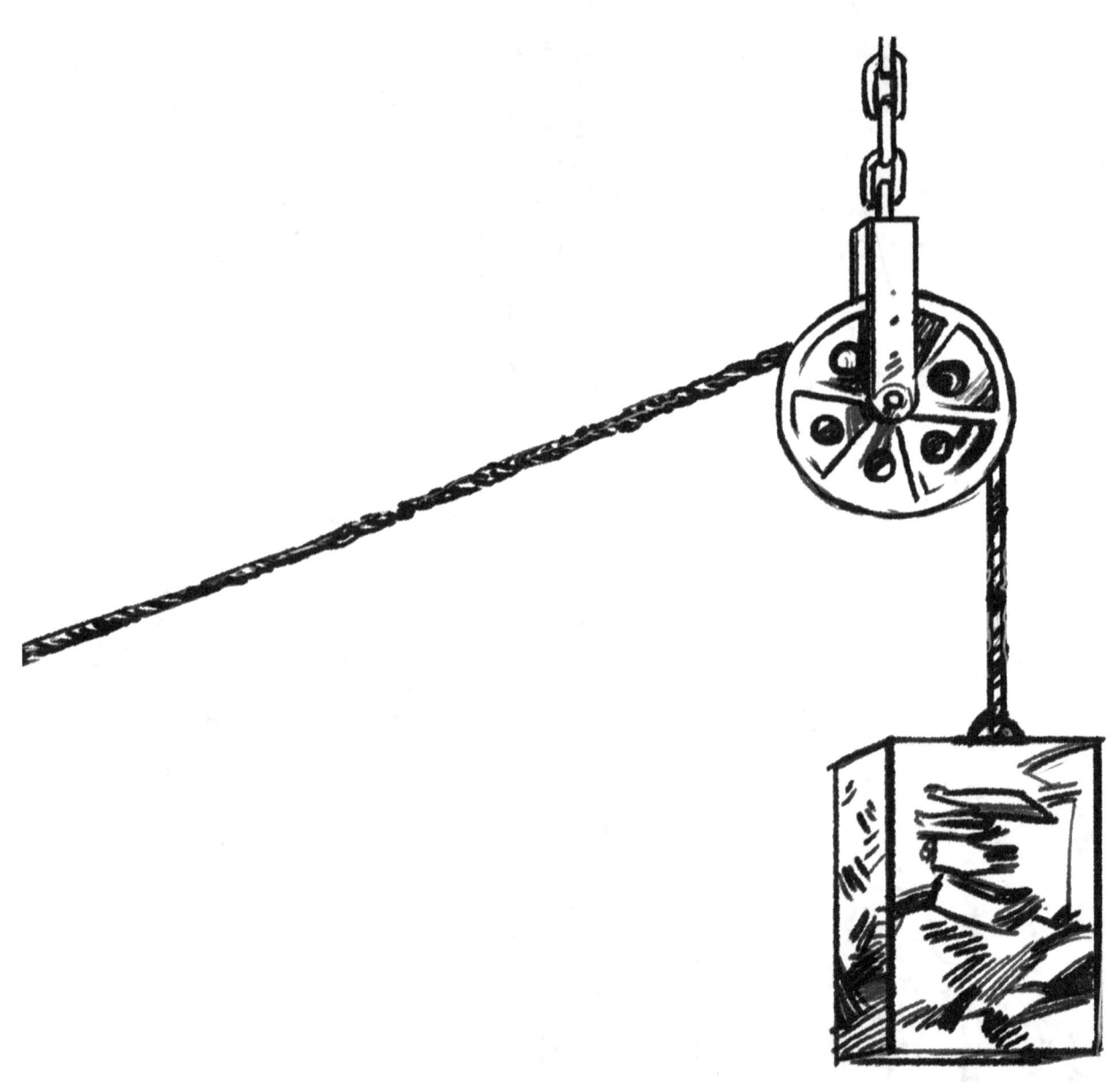

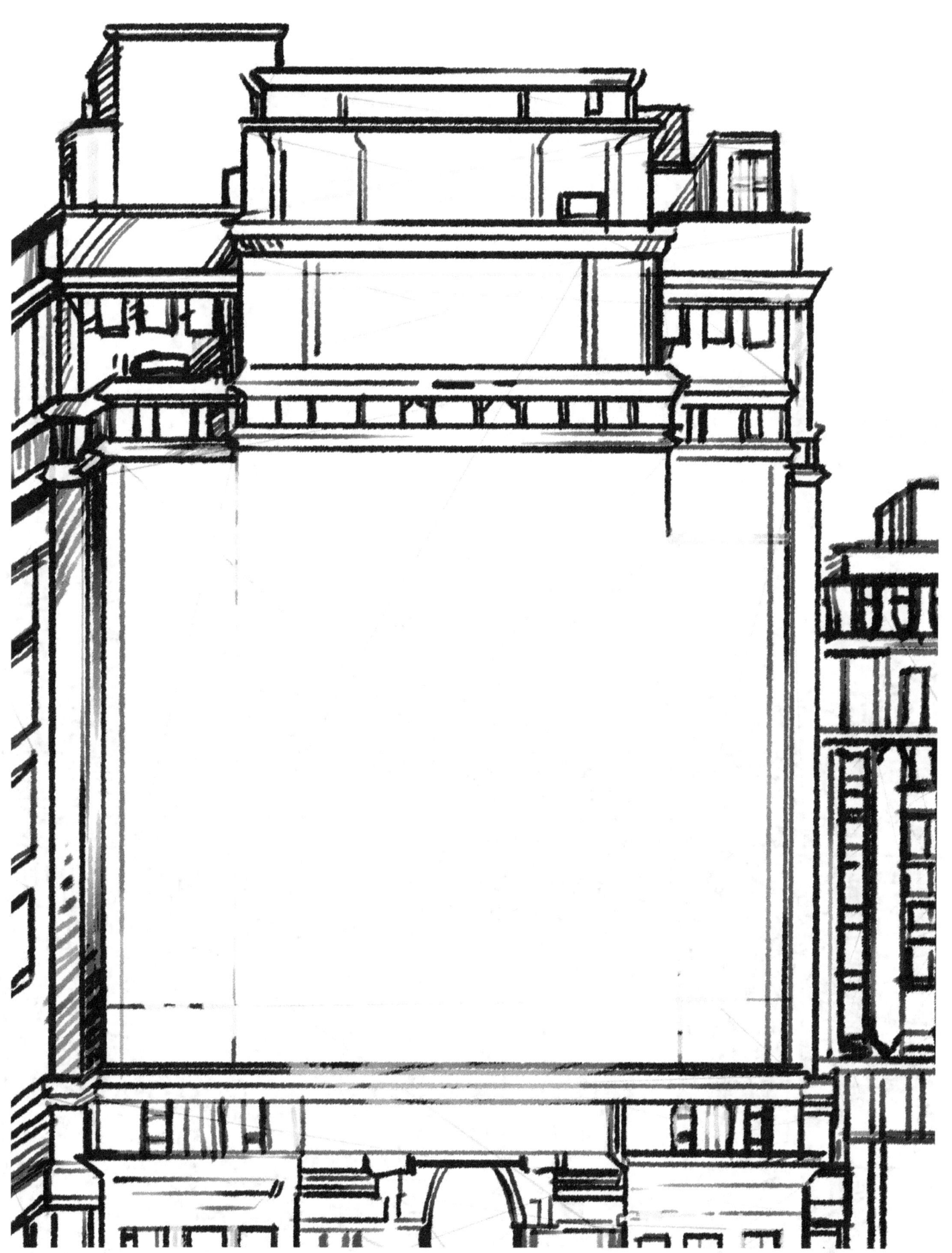

Create your own mural!

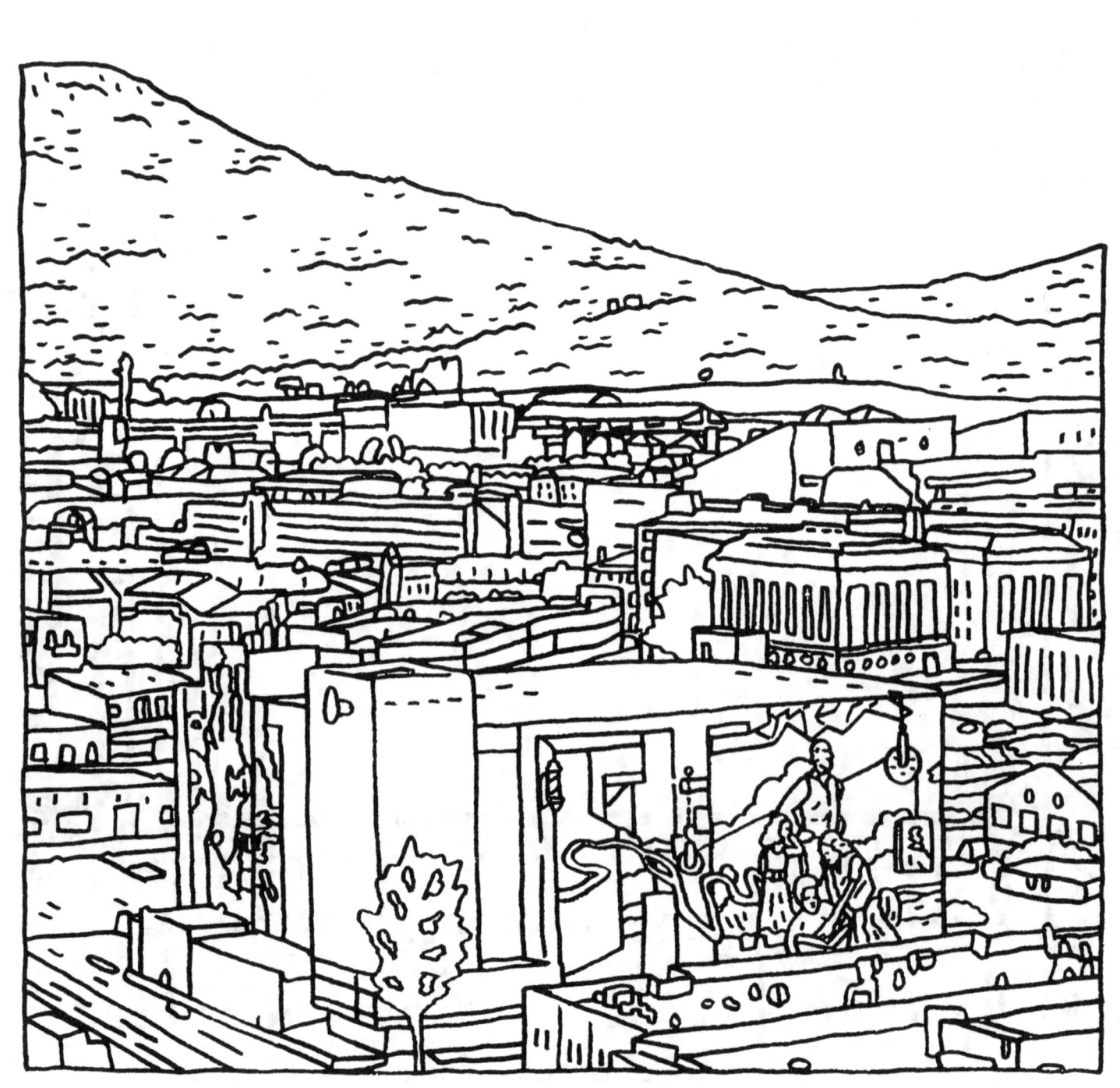

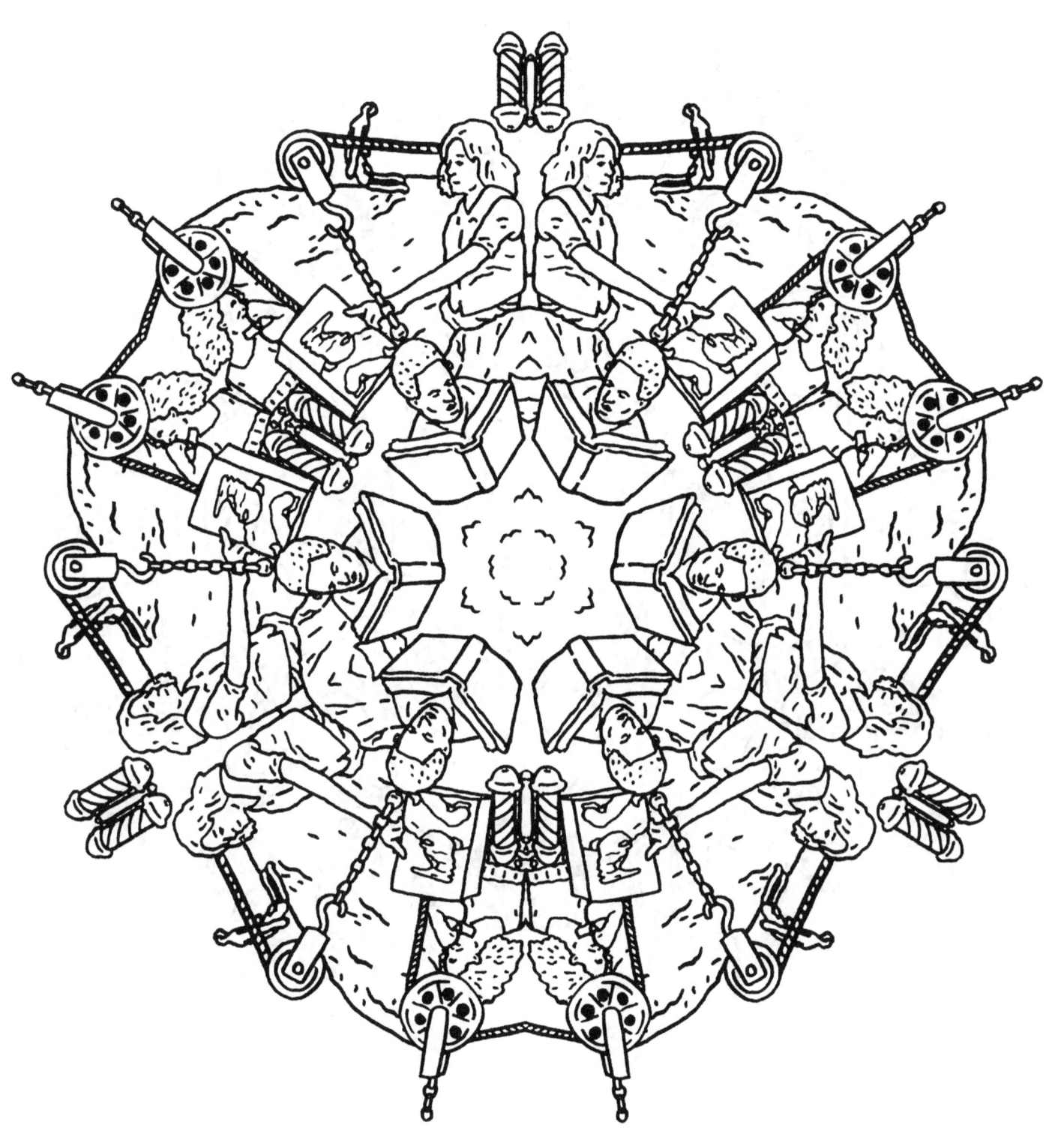

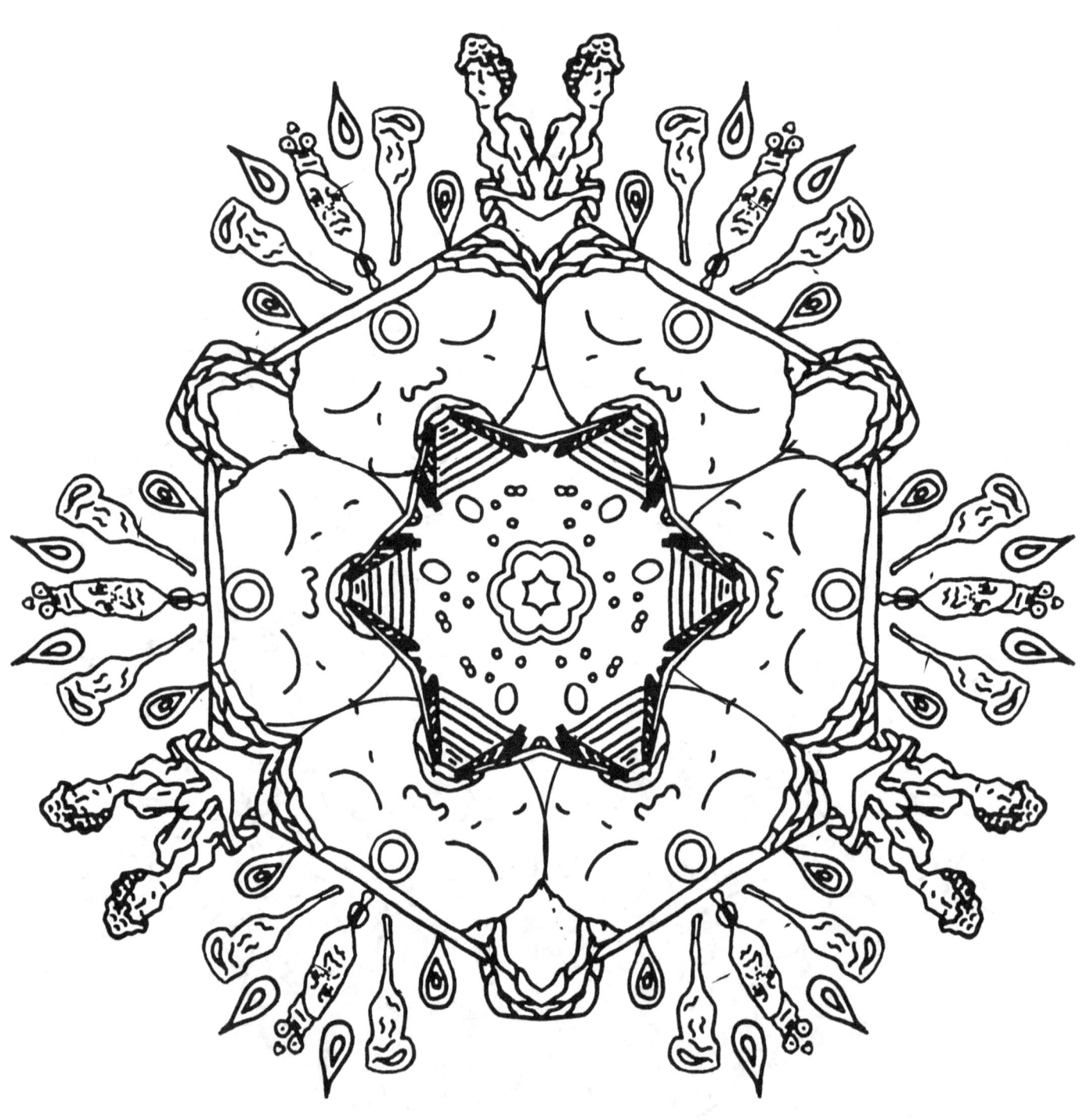

All proceeds from this book will directly fund future murals–discovering beauty with, and for communities.

Meg Saligaman Studio public commissions are done in partnership with nonprofit organizations and public agencies. Thank you for your support!

About the Artist

Meg Saligman

Originally from Olean, New York, Meg Saligman now calls Philadelphia home. Saligman's murals are considered a catalyst for the contemporary mural movement and she has painted several of the largest murals in the nation. Saligman recently created memorable installations, including *Knotted Grotto* for Pope Francis' visit to Philadelphia and *Our Common Ground* for the 2016 Republican and Democratic National Conventions.

Saligman's work has been featured by the Smithsonian American Art Museum, the New York Times, Wall Street Journal, NPR, Public Art Review, the Today Show and numerous others. She has received honors from the National Endowment for the Arts, Moore College of Art & Design, Washington University in St. Louis and Mural Arts Philadelphia.

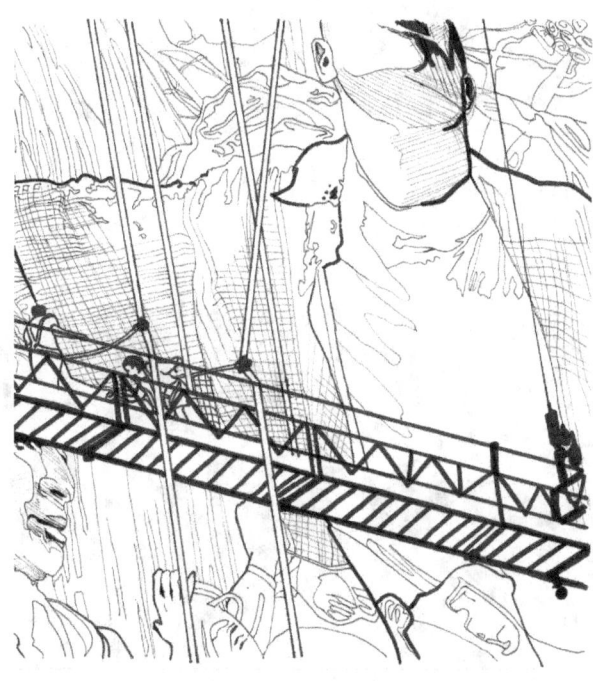

The Outliners:

Alex Derwick, the Mandala King
Illustration pages 5-8, 10-11, 16, 19-23, 26-27, 29-30, 32-33 & 36-38

Vanessa Roser
Illustration pages 4, 9, 12, 31, 34 & 35

Sofia Seidel
Illustration page 18

Meg Saligman
Illustration pages 3, 13, 15, 23 & 24,

Lizzie Kripke
Illustration Page 38

EE Yates
Illustration page 17

Acknowledgements & Thank Yous

Co-Principal Artist (Our Common Ground, We Will Not Be Satified Until, Urban Fairytale)
Lizzie Kripke

Graphic Design/Book Production
Laura Burnham & Mary Chawaga

Commissioning Agencies
Mural Arts Philadelphia - Project HOME
Sega School for Girls - Public Art Chattanooga
Shreveport Regional Arts Council

The Works

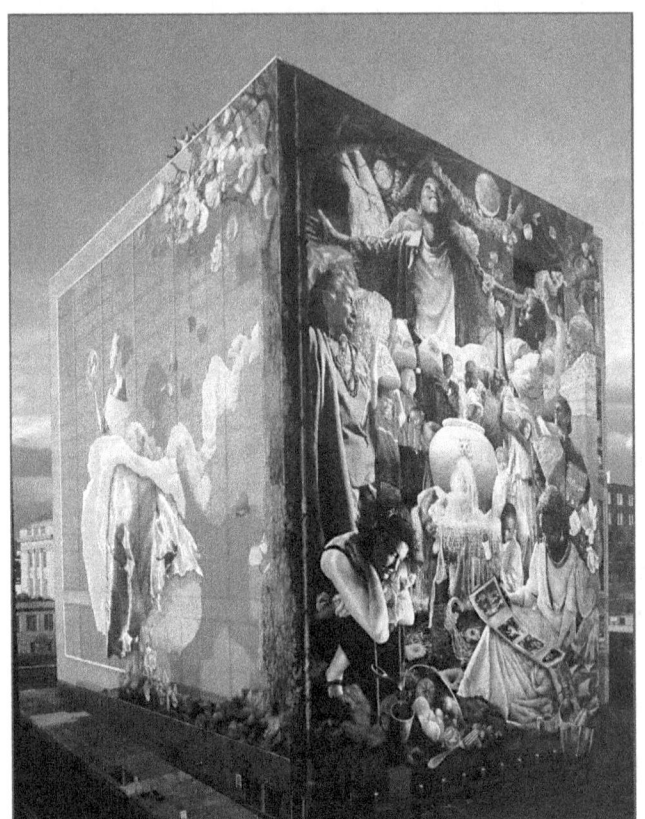

Once in a Millennium Moon
2001, Shreveport, Louisiana
30,000 Square feet

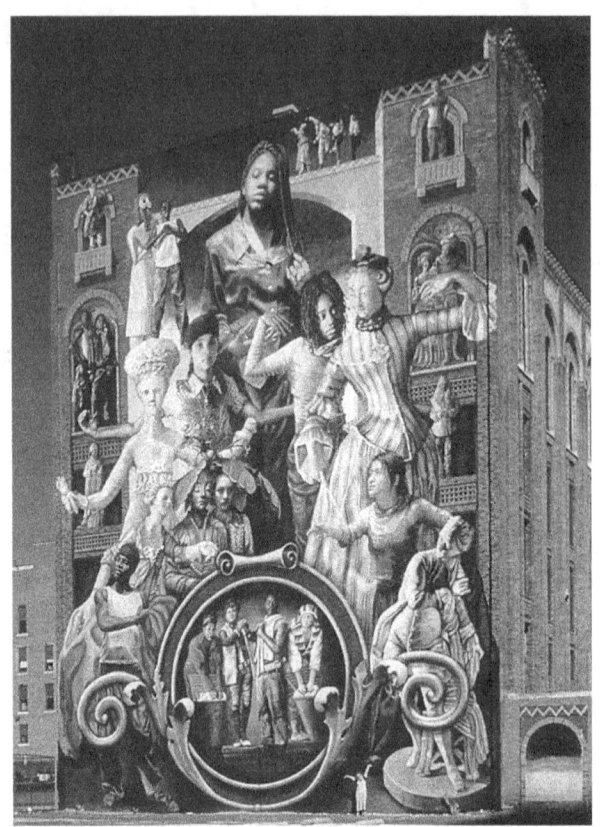

Common Threads
1998, Philadelphia PA
6,000 Square feet

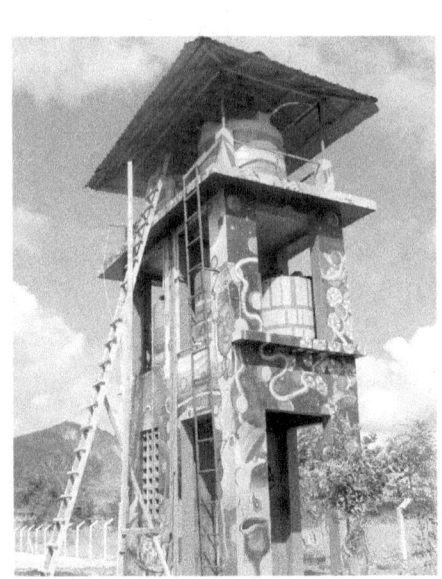

Water Tower, Water Tale
2014, Tanzania Africa
1,600 Square feet

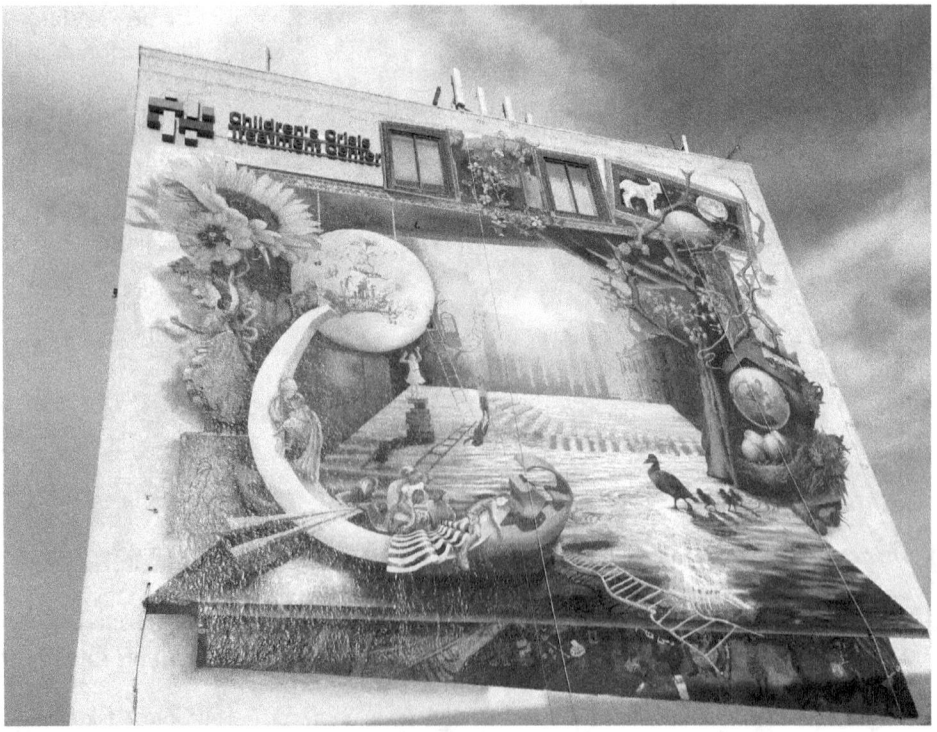

Urban Fairytale
2017, Philadelphia PA
10,000 Square feet

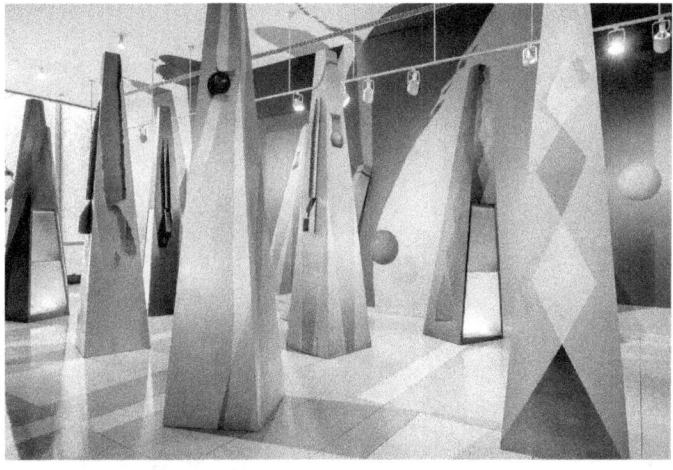

Our Common Ground
2016, Temporary installation
Republican and Democratic National Conventions
Cleveland Ohio and Philadelphia Pennsylvania

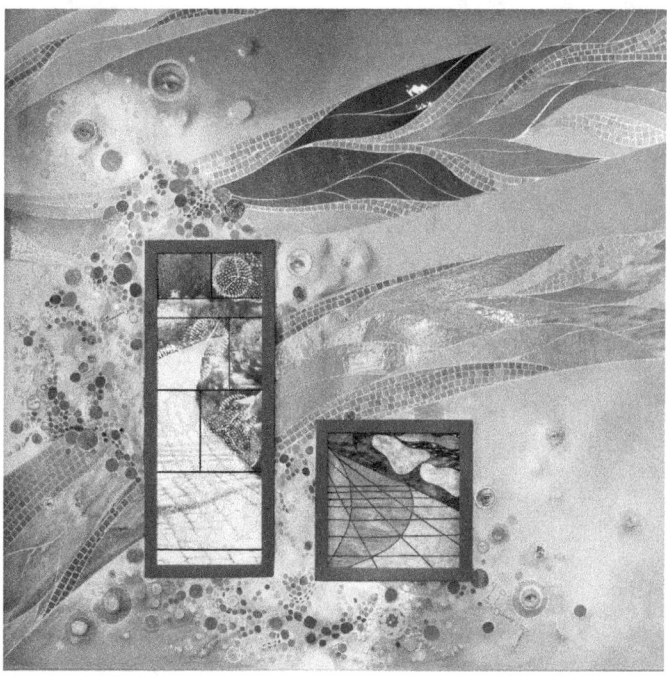

Pathways
2012, Philadelphia PA
568 Square feet

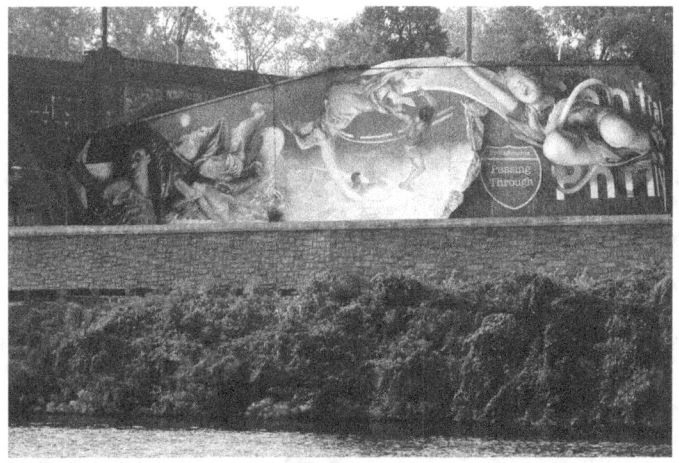

Passing Through
2004-5, Philadelphia PA
15,000 Square feet

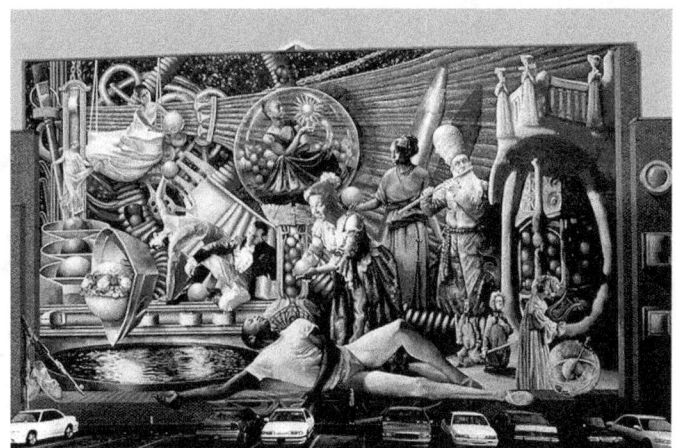

Philadelphia Muses
2004-5, Philadelphia PA
6,000 Square feet
(detail on front cover)

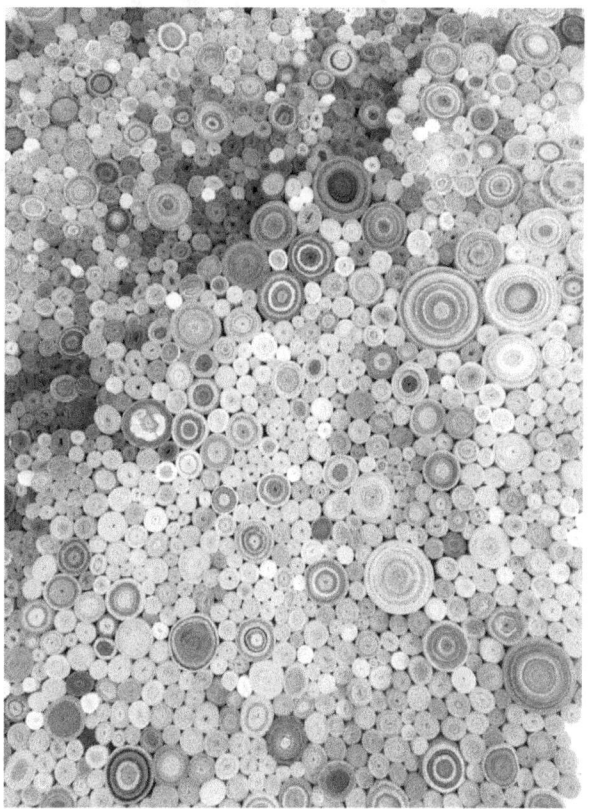

Knotted Shelter
2017, Philadephia PA
60,000 Repurposed prayer ribbons
(back cover)

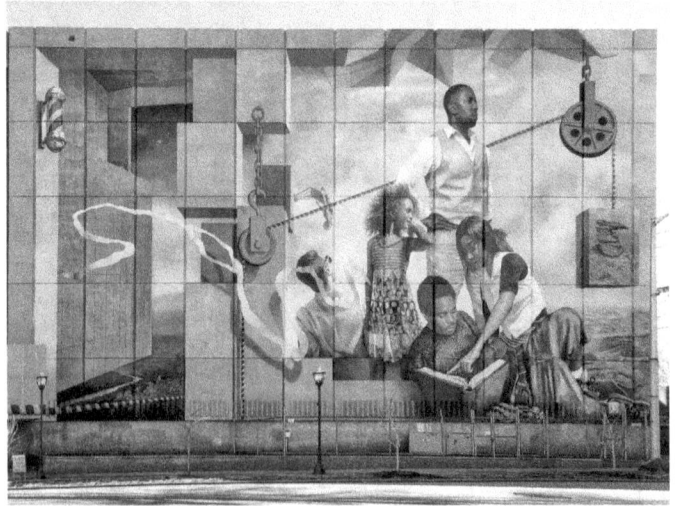

We Will Not Be Satisfied Until
2015, Chattanooga TN
42,000 Square feet

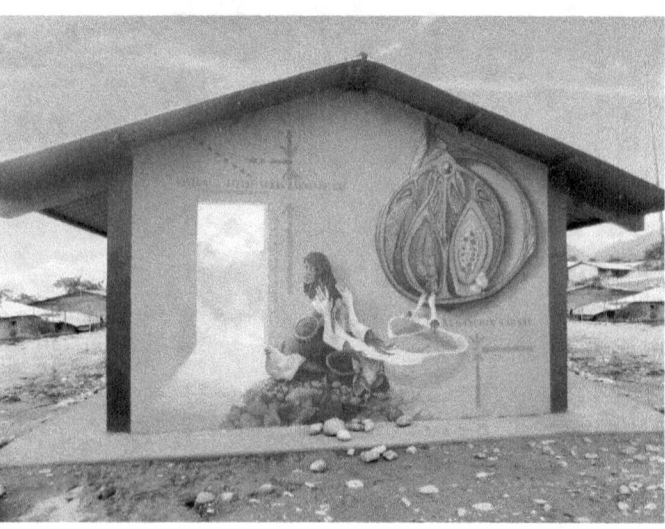

Santa Rita
2015, Santa Rita NM
600 Square feet

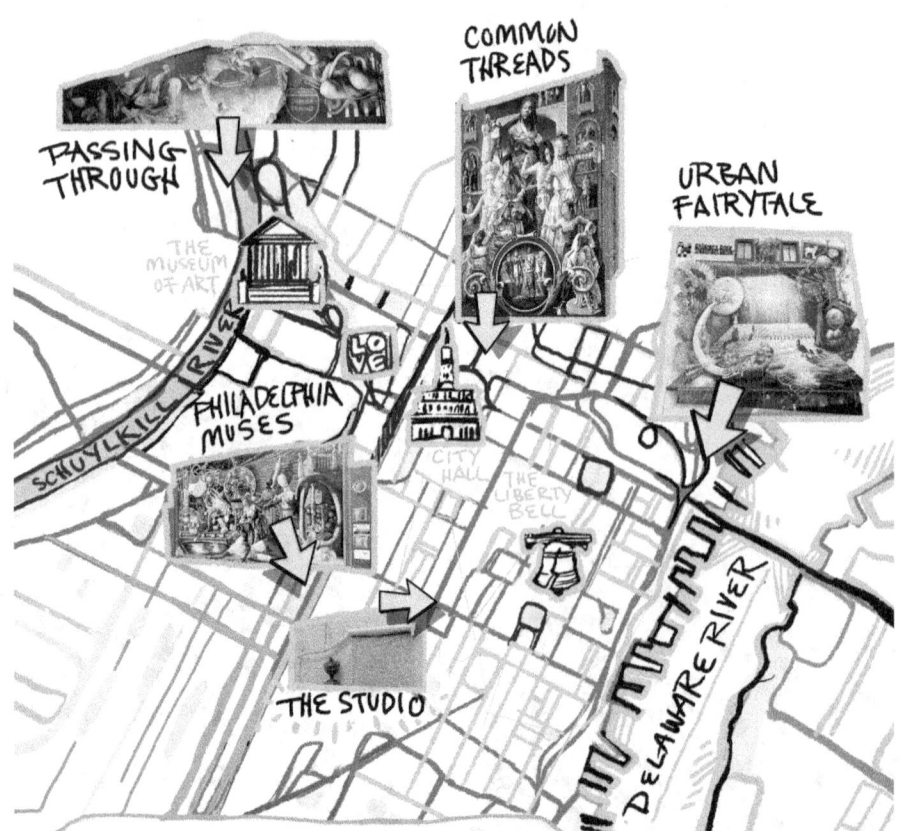

When in Philadelphia, you can visit many Meg Saligman Studio Megamurals.

For those who read to the end and want to keep the collaboration going:
Send us a self-addressed 8 x11 stamped envelope and best page.
We will incorporate your page into a future work and send you back a photo of the result.

MegaColor, 829 Banbridge Street, Philadelphia PA 19147

www.ingramcontent.com/pod-product-compliance
Lightning Source LLC
Chambersburg PA
CBHW082222220526
45470CB00010B/3280